PUFFIN BOOKS

THE CALENDAR QUIZ BOOK

A quiz book with a difference that will baffle, stimulate and entertain readers aged 10 to 14.

This lively and informative book has over 1,000 questions divided into twelve sections, one for each month of the year. Each month has four areas of questions, loosely connected with famous birthdays and anniversaries, well-known annual events or typical activities for that time of year.

Compiled by two experienced teachers, this book is full of weird and wonderful facts in every sort of quiz imaginable, accompanied by amusing cartoons. Ideal for use at home or at school, you'll wonder what you ever did without it.

Illustrated by Jane Cope

Barbara Gilgallon
and Sue Samuels

THE CALENDAR QUIZ BOOK

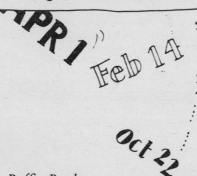

Puffin Books

Puffin Books, Penguin Books Ltd, Harmondsworth, Middlesex, England
Viking Penguin Inc., 40 West 23rd Street, New York, New York 10010, U.S.A.
Penguin Books Australia Ltd, Ringwood, Victoria, Australia
Penguin Books Canada Ltd, 2801 John Street, Markham, Ontario, Canada L3R 1B4
Penguin Books (N.Z.) Ltd, 182–190 Wairau Road, Auckland 10, New Zealand

First published 1984

Made and printed in Great Britain by
Cox & Wyman Ltd, Reading
Filmset in 10/11½ Monophoto Sabon by
Northumberland Press Ltd, Gateshead

For
James and Sam

CONTENTS

A quick quiz to get you started

Can you give the exact date or the special name for the following events?

1 **January:** Christmas decorations are traditionally taken down.
2 **February:** A day when women may leap to propose.
3 **March:** A Sunday celebration when a bunch of flowers might be given to a close relative.
4 **April:** A birthday that's the first of two!
5 **May:** A challenge trophy played for at Wembley.
6 **June:** A sporting event where love is to be avoided if you want to win the match.
7 **July:** When some swans get nicked on the Thames by Uppers.
8 **August:** A season that starts on the 'Glorious Twelfth'.
9 **September:** A quarter day and a daisy.
10 **October:** A battle, remembered on the 21st, whose hero stands tall in a London square.
11 **November:** Old crocks hurry to the seaside.
12 **December:** A day in celebration of the patron saint of children.

JANUARY

New Year's Day: *1 January*

The first of January is the beginning of the New Year – just the time to make a fresh start and do all the things you've been meaning to get around to. Here are some firsts, starting points and inventions to get you going.

13   Scattie Pattie is determined to do better this year, so she has made some New Year resolutions, but she has written them in code. What has she resolved to do?

Find the 'firsts':

14   The oldest child.
15   The opening performance of a show.
16   The help given to the injured.
17   The wife of an American president.
18   The first person to enter a home in the New Year.

19

What's the invention?

20 A way of keeping drivers to the road inspired by a feline feature.

21 A form of waterproof clothing named after its inventor.

22 A form of entertainment created from odds and ends by John Logie Baird.

23 A flushing system that so impressed Queen Elizabeth I that she ordered one for her own convenience.

24 A method of crossing the English Channel which began with two cans and a set of kitchen scales.

25

It starts like this – but what's next?

26 S, M, T, W, T, —, —.

27 Wilson, Heath, Wilson, —, —.

28 ½, 1, 2, 5, 10, 20, —, —.

29 X, XX, XXX, —, —.

30 Capricorn, Aquarius, Pisces, —, —.

31

Who was the first ...

32 man on the moon? (His initials are N.A.)

33 British woman to become Prime Minister? (M.T.)

34 man to cross Niagara Falls on a tightrope? (C.B.)

35 man to run a mile in under four minutes? (R.B.)

36 woman to fly on the space shuttle? (S.R.)

37

A quiet quiz

After all the recent festivities you might be feeling in need of a peaceful evening! Try this quiz to calm you down.

Who slept ...

38 in the Catskill Mountains and woke up to find the world completely changed?

39 for a hundred years and was awoken by a prince's kiss?

40 under a haycock while the cows and sheep went astray?

41 uncomfortably on twenty mattresses and eiderdowns?

42 in Baby Bear's bed?

43 while Jack ran off with the magic harp?

44 in Lilliput, and woke to find himself tied to the ground?

Who ...

45 dreamt that she had fallen down a rabbit hole?

46 was sent to bed in his wolf suit and visited the Land of the Wild Things?

47 lay in wait for a little girl in her granny's bed?

48 was the tiredest of the seven dwarfs?

49 had an 'Amazing Technicolor Dreamcoat'?
50 ran through the town in his nightgown?
51 dreamt of a 'White Christmas'?

Which or what ...

52 fly causes sleeping sickness?
53 does a somnambulist do?
54 is the difference between a local and a general anaesthetic?
55 do we call someone who is unable to sleep?
56 of these animals hibernates – a dormouse, a vole or a shrew?
57 lullaby tells what happens to a cradle in a tree?
58 does it mean to hypnotize someone?

59 Can you name the five beds in the picture?

Australia Day: 26 January

The first British settlement in Australia was founded on 26 January 1788 when Captain Arthur Phillip arrived to take up his post as Governor of a new penal colony. He selected the site of Sydney, now a modern and flourishing city, which people *choose* to emigrate to! Today is a public holiday to commemorate the founding of the colony.

Here are some questions to test your knowledge of Australia.

What ...

60 is the world's largest monolith?
61 is the 1,600 km barrier off the north-east coast?
62 discovery in 1851 helped triple the population in ten years?
63 is the oldest and largest Australian city, which also has an unusual opera house?
64 name is given to large, unpopulated inland areas?

Which animal or bird ...

65 is called a bear but isn't and is fond of eucalyptus leaves?
66 is also known as a laughing jackass?
67 leaps along on large hind legs and can be 2.5 metres long from nose to tail?
68 has a duck's beak, a beaver's tail and lays eggs?
69 is the second largest bird in the world, but can't fly?

Who or what ...

70 inhabited Australia before the Europeans arrived?
71 school might you attend if your home was very remote...
72 ... and what service would you depend on if you became ill?

73 prize is associated with England versus Australia Test Matches?

74 does 'Waltzing Matilda' mean?

See if you can solve these clues. The boomerang should give you a flying start!

75 The capital city of Australia.

76 A mountain range in the south-east.

77 An Aboriginal journey.

78 An island in the south.

79 A wool-producing animal.

80 Many Australian animals are of this type.

81 A day of remembrance for the landing in Gallipoli in 1915.

82 A famous surfing beach.

83 Once a jolly one camped by a billabong!

Anna Pavlova's birthday: 31 January

Anna Pavlova, one of the most famous ballerinas of all time, was born in 1885. The dance of the Dying Swan in *Swan Lake* was created especially for her. Whatever your taste in dance, from folk dancing to disco, this quiz will keep you on your toes!

Which dance . . .
84   is performed by men with bells tied around their legs?
85   from Spain involves toe and heel clicking and the use of castanets?
86   is traditionally associated with mariners?
87   was orginally danced by Hawaiian women?
88   popular in the 1920s, has the name of an American city?

What . . .
89   is a tutu?
90   is a choreographer?
91   is dancing on points?
92   tells you which foot to put your new ballet shoe on?
93   are leg warmers worn for?

Which ballet tells the story . . .
94   of Princess Odette and a spell that can only be broken when a man promises to love her forever?
95   of Swanhilde and her impersonation of a clockwork doll?
96   of Clara's visit to a magical kingdom of sweets?
97   of some famous little creatures such as Mrs Tiggy-winkle?
98   of three puppets who are brought to life at a fair?

Who ...

99 danced in *Swine Lake* with Miss Piggy?

100 danced with the Royal Ballet as a cat and created *Dash*?

101 became President of the Royal Academy of Dancing and a Dame of the British Empire?

102 danced while singin' in the rain?

103 was the American who danced barefoot in Greek tunics?

104 Can you guess the names of these dances?

FEBRUARY

Save your energy!

Dark, cold February days really make you feel like turning on the lights and sitting by a fire. Do you know how easy it is to waste energy? Test your knowledge with the game overleaf. All you need is a counter and a coin to flip. Heads move forward one place; tails two. If you land on a question box you move forward one place for a correct answer to the questions below. The object is to move the electricity from the power station to the house as quickly as possible, using as little energy as you can – apart from brain power that is!

105 If you rub a balloon on your jumper and then press it against the ceiling, what makes it stay there?

106 What animal did James Watt use to measure power?

107 Who discovered lightning was a form of electricity?

108 What colour is the live wire in a three-pin plug?

109 What element is usually used in the production of nuclear energy?

110 What source of energy is used in a hydro-electric power station?

111 What would give you more energy – twenty lettuces or a small steak?

112 This friendly robot would help you if he could but he has a problem. Can you restore his vertical line facility and work out his message?

St Valentine's Day: *14 February*

St Valentine's association with sweethearts is probably accidental. In fact there were two St Valentines, both martyred in Rome on 14 February. The linking of their feast day with courtship is more likely to be connected with springtime and events in nature than with either saint.

First, some love-ly questions!

113 Where is your love line?

114 How would you traditionally sign a Valentine card?

115 What happened to a person shot by one of Cupid's arrows?

116 Who kissed the girls and made them cry?

117 Who abolished St Valentine's Day?

118 What child is said to be 'loving and giving'?

119 You may see these initials on your Valentine envelope. What do they mean? S.W.A.L.K. and H.O.L.L.A.N.D.

Weddings:

120 On which finger are engagement and wedding rings usually worn?

121 Apart from 'something old and something new' what does a bride traditionally wear?

122 What place in Scotland was popular with English elopers in the eighteenth and nineteenth centuries?

123 What did the Owl and the Pussycat do for a ring?

124 What is a wedding breakfast?

125 Which famous wedding took place on 29 July 1981?

126 How many years of marriage are celebrated on a silver wedding anniversary?

Which . . .

127 scarecrow loves Aunt Sally?

128 Italian star was the most famous lover of the silent screen?

129 couple lived in the Garden of Eden?

130 Indian monument was built in loving memory of a Shah's wife?

131 ill-fated couple are associated with *Wuthering Heights*?

132 outlaw was Maid Marion's legendary companion?

133 flying hero was loved by Lois Lane?

134 Who's in love? Can you work out the famous couples?

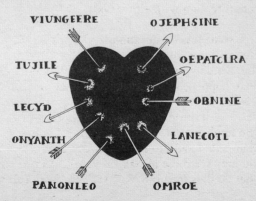

If you're under the weather

February can be the coldest and most miserable month and you may catch a cold or, worse still, 'flu. If you do, now's the time to find out what else you know about your body – besides the fact that it can sneeze!

135 Put the parts
in their places:

patella

humerus

vertebra

clavicle

ribs

pelvis

mandible

sternum

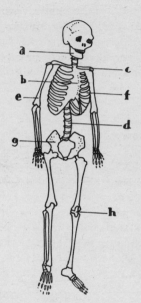

True or false?

136 Warts are caused by toads.

137 Barbers used to perform operations.

138 The pupils of your eyes get larger in dim light.

139 Your liver is your largest internal organ.

140 A balanced diet is when what you eat in the morning weighs the same as what you eat in the afternoon.

141 Colour blindness is when you can't see colours.

142 A stethoscope is used for measuring blood pressure.

143 Alexander Fleming discovered penicillin.

144 The adult human body contains enough iron to make a small nail.

145 Your intestines are five to six times as long as you are high.

146 With sudden danger your heart beats more slowly.

147 An adult's body contains about five litres of blood.

Can you believe your eyes?

148 Are the horizontal lines straight?

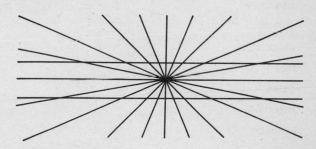

149 Who's the biggest?

Samuel Pepys's birthday: 23 *February*

Samuel Pepys was a master of the art of communication. Through his diaries we learn not only of his life but of the times he lived in. How good a communicator are you?

Which diary . . .
150 was written by a girl in hiding during the Second World War?
151 was written in secret by a boy aged 13¾?
152 thought to be sensational, was found to be a hoax in 1983?
153 recorded Edith Holden's countryside observations?
154 often contained the phrase '. . . and so to bed'?

Keeping posted:
155 Which birds were often used for carrying letters?
156 Who reorganized the postal system in 1840?
157 What form of class distinction did the Post Office introduce in 1968?
158 What does A.L.F. do?
159 What is your postcode?

Telecommunications:
160 What did Marconi do on Signal Hill, Newfoundland on 12 April 1901?
161 What was the first active communications satellite?
162 What do Goonhilly in Cornwall and Madley, Herefordshire have in common?
163 Which system uses telephone lines to transmit printed messages?
164 What is meant by a 'handle' in Citizens' Band radio jargon?

What's the connection between ...

165 a man who filled station bookstalls and a national chain of booksellers?

166 a scoop, a by-line and a leader?

167 Clark Kent, Marge Proops and Max Hastings?

168 the Light, the Third and the Home?

169 the first meal of the day and 17 January 1983?

170 What do these signs indicate?

a

b

c

d

MARCH

St David's Day: _1 March_

St David, known to the Welsh as Dewi Sant, is the patron
saint of Wales and lived in the sixth century. According to
tradition he was the son of a prince of Cardiganshire, uncle
of King Arthur and responsible for the leek becoming the
national emblem of Wales.

The answers to these questions all begin with C:
171 The Welsh name for Wales.
172 A lightweight fishing boat of ancient origin.
173 The capital city of Wales.
174 A mineral important to the Welsh economy.
175 The castle where the investiture of Prince Charles took
     place.
176 A famous rugby ground.
177 Early inhabitants of Wales.
178 A mountain range running from north to south.
179 A castle with a leaning tower, or a cheese.
180 A warm woollen jacket named after an earl.

What ...
181 mythical animal is portrayed on the Welsh flag?
182 Welsh animal tastes of cheese?
183 flower is an emblem of Wales?
184 connection is there between Wales and a two pence
     coin?
185 mountain is also known as Eryri in Wales?
186 Welsh island was a Druid stronghold?
187 earthwork formed a border between England and
     Wales?

Who ...

188 wrote *Under Milk Wood*?

189 became the ninth Princess of Wales?

190 is the famous actor born at Pontrydyfen near Port Talbot?

191 is the retired Welsh International rugby player who became head of the B.B.C.'s Outside Broadcast department?

192 was Prime Minister of Britain from 1916 to 1922?

193 was the politician who activated the National Health Service?

194 is the Welsh goon?

195 Wales is often known as the Land of Song. Can you find the missing words in these songs?

St Patrick's Day: 17 March

St Patrick, the patron saint of Ireland, is believed not to have
been Irish at all, but probably Scottish! As a boy he was cap-
tured by the Picts and sold as a slave in Ireland. Many years
later, so the story goes, he returned to Britain and decided
that he was meant to convert the Irish to Christianity. So
in honour of St Patrick, some Irish questions.

196 Ireland is sometimes known as the —————— Isle.
197 Which Irish river is the longest in the British Isles?
198 Which strange rock formation off the coast of Antrim
     was supposed to have been built by giants?
199 How is Irish coffee usually served?
200 What stone is supposed to give you the power of charm-
     ing speech if you kiss it?
201 Which Irishman tells people 'This is your life'?
202 What fuel is dug from Irish bogs?
203 What product is associated with Waterford?
204 Which town shares its name with a five-lined
     humorous verse?
205 Which Irishman wrote many plays, including
     Pygmalion?
206 What have Dana and Johnny Logan both won for
     Ireland?
207 What plant is the symbol of Ireland?
208 What are Macgillycuddy's Reeks?
209 How many types of snakes are native to Ireland?
210 What 3,000-year-old game, played with a ball and stick,
     is the national game of Ireland?
211 How many members in a Gaelic football team?
212 What musical instrument is sometimes used as an
     emblem of Ireland?
213 What is a ceilidh?
214 What is a shillelagh?

215 Can you find the missing words in these songs?
 (a) 'It's a long way to _____'.
 (b) 'When _____ eyes are smiling'.
 (c) 'And see the sun go down on _____ Bay'.
216 This fairy shoe-maker has strong associations with Ireland. Fill in the missing letters to find the name he is known by.

A quiz to do when the clocks go forward

British Summer Time was introduced in the First World War. By putting the clocks forward an hour it was possible to make the most of available daylight and save some power. The practice continued in peacetime as people enjoyed the light summer evenings. Official B.S.T. usually starts from the day following the third Saturday in March and ends on the fourth Saturday in October. This change is inclined to make people oversleep so you might find yourself doing this quiz in a hurry. The idea is to score your points in as short a time as possible. Take a deep breath and start!

217 How many days did the pease porridge stay in the pot?
218 When did Cinderella's coach turn back into a pumpkin?

219 What is the third letter from the end of the alphabet?

220 How many centimetres in 3 metres?

221 What does the 24-hour-clock show at 10 p.m.?

222 Which day did Solomon Grundy get married on?

223 Which of these is a leap year: 1800, 1900, 2000?

224 Which month is named after Julius Caesar?

225 Which two colours mixed together make orange?

226 What does G.M.T. stand for?

227 How many cards are there in a full pack, excluding jokers?

228 How many threes are in 999?

229 How many legs is a centipede thought to have?

230 How many sides has an octagon?

231 How many wives had Henry VIII?

232 How many hundreds in a million?

233 What does V.A.T. mean?

234 Whose picture is on a £5 note?

235 How many men went up the hill with the Grand Old Duke of York?

236 What are time and tide said to do?

237 Which season is called the 'Fall' in America?

238 What goes around at 33⅓ revolutions per minute?

239 How long did it take Phileas Fogg to go round the world in a balloon?

240 What sort of clock has a bird to announce the hours?

241 Which European country has long been associated with clock-making?

242 The first clock is three hours faster than the second which is four hours slower than the third which is two hours faster than the time the mouse ran up the clock. What time should they all show?

Easter

'Eastre' was originally a festival held in honour of Eostre, the goddess of dawn. The name was adopted for the Christian Paschal festival and became Easter. Eggs, lambs and other young animals are a symbol of new life and are traditionally associated with Easter and springtime.

Which rabbit or hare ...

243 lost his little blue jacket in Mr MacGregor's garden?
244 is a comic character with outstanding incisors?
245 had a sticky time with a Tar-baby?
246 was the host at a Mad Tea Party?
247 might leave you an Easter egg?
248 had a brother called Fiver who foresaw danger coming to Sandleford warren?

What sort of egg ...

249 sat on a wall?
250 denotes an intellectual person?
251 is laid in other birds' nests?
252 laid by a goose, brought wealth?
253 is said to be 'good in parts'?
254 was laid by an extinct bird?

Eastertide:

255 *Mardi gras* means Fat Tuesday. What is traditionally eaten on this day in Britain?

256 Ash Wednesday is the first day of Lent. How did it get its name?

257 The forty days of Lent are said to correspond to forty days of Christ's life. Where and how did He spend them?

258 On Maundy Thursday the sovereign distributes money to men and women who have rendered Christian service. What is special about it?

259 Good Friday is the anniversary of the Crucifixion. Why is Friday the thirteenth said to be particularly unlucky?

260 Spot the six differences:

The mothers, fathers and young have become separated. Can you fit the families together?

261 cob   doe   gosling
262 gander   mare   lamb
263 buck   duck   cygnet
264 ram   pen   foal
265 stallion   goose   duckling
266 drake   ewe   fawn

How eggspert are you?

267 Put the eggs in order.

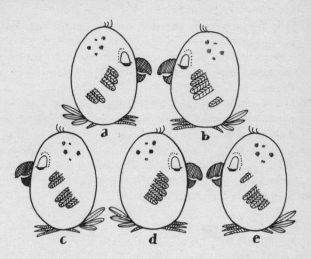

268 Which is the odd egg out?

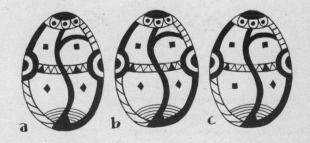

APRIL

1 April is eagerly awaited by those who like to get up to mischief. In France an April fool is *un poisson d'Avril*, in Scotland a *gowk* or a *cuckoo*. You certainly have to keep your wits about you but be sure to do all your pranks before midday as that is when foolery officially ends. You may have to look twice at this quiz – it isn't all it seems to be.

269 Where are fools said to rush in?

270 When did the Piltdown man live?

271 What colour is a blue tit's breast?

272 What sort of building is a folly?

273 What does a miser spend and a spendthrift save?

274 In which year do Christmas Day and New Year's Day fall in the same year?

275 How did foolscap paper get its name?

276 At which banquet in 1597 did Henry VIII eat three whole geese?

277 What is a Bombay duck?

278 Who would use a zoomer and a waggler?

279 Where do squirrels lay their eggs?

280 Who would use a tree-shaker?

281 Where do marsh-mallows grow?

282 Muckle John was thought to be the last court jester. Which king did he amuse?

283 Where in a garden might you find a ha-ha?

284 How do you milk a pigeon?

285 What is elbow grease used for?

286 Whose footprints are these:

287 Who was the 'wisest fool in Christendom'?

288 When did a Bikini explode?

289 Can a kangaroo jump higher than a house?

290 When was Wednesday, 2 September followed by Thursday, 14 September?

291 Which of these clowns is the odd one out? If you can sort out the letters they are juggling you will find a character from Harlequinade.

William Shakespeare's birthday: 23 April

Shakespeare was born in Stratford-upon-Avon in 1564. As a young man he went to London, joined a company of actors and was soon writing plays as well as acting in them. These tragedies, comedies and histories are world famous 400 years later. Celebrate the birthday of the greatest English dramatist by attempting these 'entertaining' questions.

These titles have all been slightly altered. Can you say what they should be?

292 *Mickbeth.*
293 *A Midsummer Day's Dream.*
294 *Romeo and Harriet.*
295 *Julia Caesar.*
296 *Hamlet, Prince of Norway.*

297 Try to correct these misquotes and then match them to the right play above:
   (a) 'Beware the tides of March'.
   (b) 'Something is forgotten in the state of Denmark'.
   (c) 'Double, double boil and bubble'.
   (d) 'Romeo, Romeo where's your cart now, Romeo?'
   (e) 'I know a bunk whereon the wild thyme blows'.

What form of entertainment is performed ...

298 silently?
299 in a ring with animals and jugglers?
300 with men playing dames and a girl the principal boy?
301 on a beach in a striped tent?
302 at Oberammergau every ten years?

Which theatre ...

303 in Southwark was the original venue for many of Shakespeare's plays?

304 in Warwickshire is famous for its Shakespearian productions?

305 is the base of the Royal Shakespeare Company in London?

306 is really three theatres on the South Bank of the Thames?

307 in the open air would you find near London Zoo?

308 Who are these five stars of the stage with muddled surnames? There are three women and two men. They all share the mystery letter in the middle.

St George's Day: *23 April*

St George is the patron saint of England. Nobody knows exactly who he was, but it is generally accepted that he was a Roman soldier martyred about A.D. 300. The legend of St George slaying the dragon is a story to show the triumph of good over evil.

Which town or city is ...

309 furthest north: Newcastle, Middlesbrough or Durham?

310 furthest south: Birmingham, Leicester or Northampton?

311 furthest east: Cambridge, Colchester or Canterbury?

312 furthest west: Liverpool, Crewe or Bristol?

313 History has got into a muddle. Can you arrange these events into their proper order?

    (a) Gainsborough paints 'The Blue Boy'.

    (b) Florence Nightingale lights her lamp in the Crimea.

    (c) Henry VIII marries his third wife.

    (d) The shilling in your purse becomes 5p.

    (e) Virginia Wade wins the Ladies' Singles at Wimbledon.

    (f) Hadrian builds a wall.

    (g) Lady Godiva goes for a ride.

    (h) Drake plays bowls at Plymouth.

Who ...

314 was made Chief Scout of the world in 1920?

315 received the D.B.E. in 1965 for her abstract carving in wood and stone?

316 wrote about Little Lord Fauntleroy and a secret garden?

317 made pottery and gave his name to a shade of blue?

318 saw a 'host of golden daffodils'?

319 wrote about pride and prejudice?

What are these tourist attractions?

320 City of springs in which you ought to be clean.

321 East Anglian area noted for boating and birds.

322 City where you could be ignored, but everybody notices the cathedrals, both old and new.

323 Pointed protuberances off the Isle of Wight.

324 In Cumbria, pikes, hikes and plenty of water.

325 Circles of stone on Salisbury Plain.

326 These Morris dancers are dying for dinner. Combine the words to find out what regional specialities they are going to eat.

A day trip to Boulogne

Bonjour mes enfants! Pour vous lucky ones qui viennent sur un day trip to Boulogne ce mois, voilà quelques choses! Aussi, un interesting fact pour vous: 'La Marseillaise' (la national anthem) was composée ce mois in 1792. Vous live et learn, n'est-ce pas?

What do these have in common?
327 Brie, Port Salut, Camembert.
328 Chanel, Saint Laurent, Dior.
329 Calais, Boulogne, Dieppe.
330 Peugeot, Citroën, Renault.
331 Quasimodo, Astérix, the Count of Monte Cristo.
332 Beaujolais, chablis, champagne.
333 Monet, Matisse, Renoir.
334 Baguette, croissant, brioche.

What is associated with ...

335 Grasse?
336 Cordon Bleu?
337 Dijon?
338 Le Mans?
339 Vichy?
340 Limoges?

Tour de Paris:

A famous cycle race, the Tour de France, takes place every year in July. About 150 cyclists ride 3,000 miles round the perimeter of France. You have to be fit to take part! If you're not feeling quite so energetic, have a go at this armchair Tour de Paris instead. Just identify the landmarks on your journey. Start on the outskirts of Paris at 341 ...

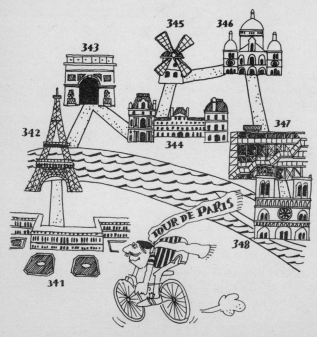

341 a great palace with beautiful gardens built for Louis
     XIV. Then continue past:
342 a steel tower on four legs, made for the Centennial
     Exposition in 1889.
343 an arch beneath which the Unknown Soldier rests.
344 once a palace, now a famous gallery which contains
     the 'Mona Lisa'.
345 a windmill famous for the can-can.
346 a white church with many domes, on a hill in
     Montmartre.
347 a contemporary arts centre of unusual design, featuring
     tubed escalators outside.
348 a famous Gothic cathedral on the Île de la Cité.

MAY

May Day is traditionally celebrated by dancing around a maypole and gathering garlands of flowers. The Anglo-Saxons called May the month of flowers and it is certainly a time when nature is very much in evidence. It is also recognized as an international holiday to celebrate Labour Day.

Fill in the answers to the nature trail on this special crossword. The last letter of each word will begin the next.

349 Maidens wash in this on May Day morning.

350 Water-loving tree said to weep.

351 Insect with a slender waist and a nasty sting.

352 Bird found on Lundy Island and on the cover of this book.

353 Plant with leaves that sting.

354 Tree which may be attacked by a Dutch disease.

355 Another name for the hawthorn which blossoms this month.

356 Tree often found in churchyards.

357 Bird that pecks at the bark of trees for food.

358 Small bird with a red breast.

359 Plant whose deadly variety is known as *Belladonna*.

360 The name given to a spike of corn.

361 Another name for a mountain ash tree.

362 Here we go gathering _ _ _ _ in May.

363 High-flying bird that lays its eggs on the ground.

364 A bird of prey like a small falcon.

365 Insect instructed by the rhyme to 'fly away home'.
366 Flower once known as the 'day's eye'.
367 Bird whose cry sounds like 'a little bit of bread and no cheese'.
368 Large grass that grows near water and can be used to make music.

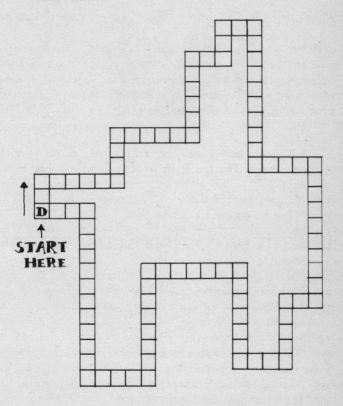

D

START HERE

369 Link the names to find out who's doing the Floral Dance round the maypole!

A *fancy dress party*

In the month of May Queens and Morris dancers, many people are dressing up, despite the old adage 'Ne'er cast a clout till May be out' (clout is an item of clothing, not a clout round the ear!).

370 Mary Poppins, Cleopatra, Aunt Sally, Sherlock Holmes, Bonnie Prince Charlie and Henry VIII have been invited to a fancy dress party. Instead of making a special costume, they have decided to swap around their hats, clothes and shoes. Who did they lend their outfits to?

MARY   CHARLIE   HENRY

CLEOPATRA   SHERLOCK   SALLY

Now address yourself to these questions.

Who wore ...

371 a hat a hundred and two feet wide?

372 a suit of new clothes that turned him into a laughing stock?

373 a dress that turned to rags at midnight?

What are ...

374 bustles?

375 boas?

376 bell-bottoms?

Why would you wear ...
377 hoops?
378 pattens?
379 spatterdashes?

When ...
380 did Amelia display her bloomers?
381 did Dior's 'New Look' arrive?
382 did the mini skirt first become popular?

Where would you wear ...
383 a pork pie?
384 mutton chops?
385 a leg of mutton?

Golden oldies!

May gets its name from either Maia, the goddess of
growth, or from 'maiores' meaning elders, in honour of old
people. To give you a rest from answering questions, here
are some for you to ask any tame adults who are sitting about
looking bored!

Complete the line:
386 It was an itsy bitsy teeny weeny ...
387 Does your chewing gum ...
388 You push the damper in ...
389 She wore red feathers ...
390 Mares eat oats and does eat oats ...

Who said ...
391 'I want to be alone'.
392 'If she can stand it, I can. Play it!'
393 'Come up some time and see me'.

394 'Wakey wakey!'
395 'Hello, playmates!'

Who was the partner?
396 Bill and —.
397 The Lone Ranger and —.
398 Laurel and —.
399 — and Doris Waters.
400 — and Costello.

Who was . . .
401 the Sweater Girl?
402 the Oomph Girl?
403 the Kid?
404 I.T.M.A.?
405 the Ole Groaner?

406 What were the Black Bottom, the Twist, the Hokey Cokey, the Palais Glide and the Tango? (Win an extra point for a demonstration of each!)
407 Who sang these Golden Oldies? And in which year were they at number one in the hit parade?

Do you have a good head for heights?

408 If you have the energy, see if you can identify these
volcanic mountains by sorting out the letters.

On 29 May 1953 the Union Jack was placed on the summit
of Mount Everest. In this quiz we challenge you to reach some
dizzying heights. As you get nearer to the summit the
questions get harder but you can gain more points. Good
climbing! Questions 409–413 earn 1 point, 414–418 earn two
points, 419–423 earn three points.

Start at the bottom and work your way up.

423 How high is Mount Everest?

422 Name the highest mountain in Africa.

421 What do Simplon, St Bernard and St Gotthard have in common?

420 If the temperature gets lower as you ascend, why do skiers get sunburnt?

419 You are now crossing the snowline. What is it?

418 Which two countries are separated by the Pyrenees?

417 What is the longest mountain range in the world?

416 What do you call the mountain home of an eagle?

415 Which Roman god gave his name to volcanoes?

414 What is the highest mountain in Wales?

413 What mountain flower did the Von Trapp family sing about?

412 Who crossed the Alps with the aid of some elephants?

411 Who accompanied Sir Edmund Hillary to the summit of Everest in 1953?

410 Who led the children of Hamelin into the mountain, never to be seen again?

409 Which Swiss mountain girl did Joanna Spyri write about?

JUNE

Derby Day

The Derby, held at Epsom in Surrey, is regarded as the highlight of the horse-racing calendar. It was established by the twelfth Earl of Derby in 1780 and the first winner was Diomed. The race is for three-year-old colts and fillies only and is one of the classic races: the others are the Oaks, the St Leger, the 1,000 Guineas and the 2,000 Guineas.

So, under starter's orders . . . race away!

Which horse . . .
424 was made a Roman consul by his owner, Caligula?
425 had a Grand National hat trick?
426 gallops through the sky?
427 in Berkshire is about 360 feet from nose to tail and never moves?
428 carried her rider from London to York?
429 was darkly good looking?

What . . .
430 is the Jockey Club?
431 is steeplechasing?
432 sport resembles hockey on horseback?
433 cowboy competition may include riding bucking broncos?
434 prevents a horse from winning the Derby more than once?
435 person completed this 1976 Olympic team: Richard Meade, Hugh Thomas, Lucinda Green?

436 Connect the kit:

saddle	pick
hoof	brush
dandy	comb
curry	soap

437 Label these parts of the horse: muzzle, mane, withers, croup, fetlock, forelock, hock, elbow, cannon.

Which breed or type of horse ...

438 according to Bedouin legend, was created from a handful of the south wind?

439 is used at the Spanish Riding School in Vienna?

440 is the largest heavy horse?

441 most used in harness, gives its name to a vehicle for hire?

442 is golden in colour, with a flaxen mane and tail?

443 once used by American Indians, is sometimes known as a 'painted horse'?

SPOTTED DICK   NIGHT RIDER   FLASH HARRY   GREY GHOST

444 Which jockey is riding which horse?
Mo Jersey is younger than Piggy Lister, and Piggy was born after Wally Kitson. Neville Starkers is not as old as Piggy but older than Mo. Night Rider is ridden by the oldest jockey. Mo's horse does not have a blaze on its face. Piggy's horse is not a grey. Neville's horse is not spotted. The grey is ridden by the youngest jockey.

The Queen's official birthday

The Queen celebrates two birthdays – one private and one public. She follows a custom that began in 1805 when a special parade was held on George III's birthday. This ceremony, known as Trooping the Colour, involves the display of a regiment's banner on Horse Guards Parade. It is always held on a Saturday in June, no matter which day the monarch's birthday really falls on, as the weather is more likely to be fine at this time of year.

Which member of the present Royal Family ...
445 was born in Corfu?
446 lived in a house called Althorp as a child?

447 has written a children's story about an ancient Scottish gentleman?
448 is second in line to the throne?
449 was involved in the war in the South Atlantic in 1982?

Which monarch ...
450 lost his treasure in the Wash?
451 lost his temper with an Archbishop and caused his murder?
452 lost his crown, a battle and his life at Bosworth?
453 lost his head at Whitehall?
454 lost his heart to Mrs Simpson and, subsequently, his throne?

Which palace or royal residence ...
455 was built by a butcher's son?
456 was built on the site of a leper colony?
457 has a Swiss cottage in which Queen Victoria's children played?
458 once housed the Royal Mint, a Royal menageric and an armourer's workshop?
459 did Marble Arch once stand in front of?

Which or what ...
460 crown is used to crown the monarch?
461 garment is Raleigh supposed to have covered a puddle with for Elizabeth I?
462 was dropped by a lady, picked up by a king and became an order?
463 Queen fled from Oxford Castle wearing white sheets?
464 style of hat does the Queen favour and why?

465 Some kings and queens have had strange nicknames. Look at these pictures and guess who they are:

Magna Carta: *15 June*

King John was persuaded to seal the Magna Carta (Great Charter) on 15 June 1215 at Runnymede near Windsor. The charter, drawn up by churchmen and barons, made the King's decisions subject to the law of the land. Although it was written so long ago, we still feel its influence today in our legal system and those of many other countries. Four original copies exist, two in the British Museum and one each in Lincoln and Salisbury Cathedrals. Try the following questions which are all to do with law.

In Britain, at what age are you . . .
466 responsible for doing up your own seat-belt?
467 able to leave school?
468 able to drive a car on a public highway?
469 able to vote?
470 able to stand for Parliament?

Which or what . . .
471 did the Metropolitan Police once use their top hats for?
472 dogs are most widely used for police work?
473 method is used to recreate suspects' faces?
474 are arch, loop and whorl?
475 might a polygraph be used for?

Which law-breaker . . .
476 was a highwayman in London and hanged in York as a horse thief?
477 made Whitechapel women afraid to go out in 1888?
478 was a barber who sometimes gave his customers more than a shave?
479 had a troop of Merry Men and lived in a forest?
480 taught little boys how to pick pockets?

Which or what . . .
481 prison was demolished to make way for the Central Criminal Court?
482 breakfast cereal do prisoners like least?
483 Quaker woman is famous for her work in prison reform?
484 prison had a 'bird-man'?
485 is parole?

486 What's the punishment?

Mystery and imagination

You might find yourself doing tests or exams this month, so here's a quiz based on problems and mysteries, real and imaginary. You may even find some inspiration for your aching brain!

Who solved the problem ...

487 of rats in Hamelin Town?
488 of her size by drinking from a bottle labelled 'Drink Me'?
489 of saving Wilbur the pig by weaving messages in her web?
490 of entering Troy by hiding in a wooden horse?
491 of an unexplained death on the Orient Express?

What mysterious ...

492 ship was discovered floating in the Azores in 1872 without her crew?
493 land in South America was said to be so full of gold that the natives threw it away?
494 creature with huge feet is said to live in the Himalayas?
495 cup was the subject of a quest by King Arthur's knights?
496 cat is called the 'Hidden Paw'?

What ingenious ...

497 creatures make use of the rubbish left on Wimbledon Common?
498 boy lives in a dump and invents things from rubbish?
499 rodents found a way of moving Mrs Frisby's house out of danger?
500 professor invents odd machines for such things as catching burglars and stroking cats?
501 creatures 'borrow' from humans and live in secret places?

Solve the secret of the triangle by answering the questions below. Fill in all the boxes, starting from the top and use the shaded letters to find the name of a mysterious triangle.

502 The code name for 007's superior.

503 The boat that Thor Heyerdahl used to test a theory.

504 A mysterious sighting in the sky.

505 Charlie ____, an oriental detective.

506 Father _____, a priest and a detective.

507 The profession of Sherlock Holmes's friend, Watson.

508 Simenon's French detective.

509 An inspector on the trail of the Pink Panther.

JULY

The eastern part of the U.S.A. belonged to Britain until 1776,
when the settlers drew up a Declaration of Independence
which stated that they wished to rule themselves. After a war
with Britain they eventually achieved their aims and George
Washington became their first president in 1779.

510 First of all, see if you can find some 'highlights' of
America advertised below:

True or False?

511 The Boston Tea Party took place in a restaurant in Massachusetts.

512 The Wall Street Crash happened when several buildings were blown up in New York.

513 The Louisiana Purchase was made by the U.S.A. when they bought the French-owned land between the Mississippi and the Rocky Mountains.

514 The Mason–Dixon Line was the first railway to run from the west to the east coast of America.

515 Calamity Jane was born Martha Canary.

516 The Statue of Liberty was given to America by the French.

517 The Ivy League is the society for the preservation of American evergreens.

518 The Gettysburg Address was the location of Abraham Lincoln's home in Pennsylvania.

Can you find out what these groups have in common?

519 Cochise, Geronimo, Victorio.

520 Colt, Deringer, Winchester.

521 Washington, Jefferson, Roosevelt, Lincoln.

522 Ho Jo's, Wendy's, McDonald's.

523 *Jaws, E.T., Close Encounters of the Third Kind.*

524 Lucy, Linus, Charlie Brown.

525 Missouri, Arkansas, Ohio.

526 Custer, Eisenhower, Haig, Patton.

527 Louisa May Alcott, Laura Ingalls Wilder, Harriet Beecher Stowe.

528 Metro-Goldwyn-Mayer, 20th-Century Fox, Paramount.

529 Freshmen, sophomores, juniors.

530 Bat Masterson, Bill Tilghman, Wyatt Earp.

St Swithin's Day: 15 July

St Swithin wanted to be buried in a churchyard so that the 'sweet rain of Heaven' could fall on his grave. When the monks decided to move the grave into the church, the removal had to be put off because it rained for forty days. They finally realized that it was best to leave the grave where it was. The superstition remains that if it rains on St Swithin's Day it will not stop for forty days.

What ...
531 is a fair-weather friend?
532 is a rain check?
533 are the water signs of the zodiac?
534 is a red sky in the morning supposed to mean?
535 are still waters said to do?
536 did Jonas Hanway hold up that made people laugh but kept his head dry?

What happens ...
537 when clouds cool down?
538 to pure water at 0° centigrade?
539 when salt water is boiled?
540 when you breathe on a cold window pane?
541 to the level of a glass of water with ice in it when the ice melts?
542 to water left on a sunny windowsill?

Where in the song or rhyme ...
543 did Doctor Foster fall in a puddle?
544 do raindrops keep falling?
545 do the rains in Spain fall?
546 did Itsy Bitsy spider get washed out?
547 did the old man go when it rained and poured?

What ...

548   uses more water – a shower or a bath?

549   makes the inside of a kettle furry?

550   happens to the water in a spin drier?

551   is sometimes added to water to help prevent tooth decay?

552   fraction of the human body is water?

553   This phenomenon's named
But its colours are not
When you've filled in the letters
What's starred for the pot?

```
        R _ _*
     _ _ A _ _ _
        I _ _ _ _ _*
  *_ _ _ _ N
        B _ _ _
     _ _ O _ _ _
  _ _ _ _*_ W
```

Sports Day

Sports Day always requires a lot of organization, but things have gone rather haywire at this one. Can you sort it out?

554 Some famous names in sport have lost some vital pieces of equipment. Can you say who has lost what?
Lucinda Green, Sebastian Coe, Chris Lloyd, Geoff Capes, Jayne Torvill, Barry Sheene.

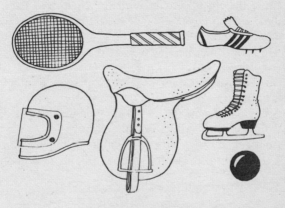

Now the scoreboard has gone wrong. With the help of these clues can you make it add up to the correct total? We need the number of ...

555 players in a netball team.
556 minutes in a game of soccer.
557 events in a decathlon.
558 red balls on a snooker table.
559 men in a rugby union side.
560 runs in a maiden over.

SCORE BOARD

137

561　These sporting terms have become muddled. Can you say whether they belong to judo, fencing, cricket, golf or tennis?

parry	googly	birdie
howzat!	bouncer	tie-break
eagle	shiai	let
deuce	hajime	riposte
dan	fore!	lunge

Bring the champions in with the chequered flag. The dark squares cover some of the letters in these famous names. Who are they?

562　The former number one woman tennis player in Britain.

563　An Austrian Formula One driver.

564　An English cricketer who has played football for Scunthorpe.

565　A British woman sprinter who won a bronze medal in the 1983 World Athletics Championship.

566　An ice-skater who won an Olympic gold medal in 1976.

567　The British women's freestyle swimming champion.

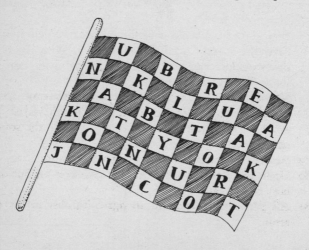

The last day of term

It's here at last! You may find that you can relax a bit today and discover that your teacher is human after all! If you wonder why he keeps grinning to himself perhaps it is because he is looking forward to the holiday as much as you are. If you can snatch a spare moment you can find out if your teacher knows the answer to these 'educational' questions.

Can you name ...

568 the naughty comic-strip characters otherwise known as the Minx, the Peril, the Dodger and the Menace?

569 a boarding school famous for its naughty girls?

570 a schoolboy known as the 'Fat Owl of the Remove'?

571 the mischievous boy who has to put up with Violet Elizabeth Bott?

572 a London comprehensive of which Tucker is a past pupil?

573 the star pupil at Fagin's school for pickpockets?

574 Darbishire's great friend at Linbury Court prep school?

575 a four-legged child whose curiosity led to a painfully elongated nose?

576 the boy who played truant and was turned into a donkey?

577 the 'worst schoolgirl in the world'?

These are some rather posh descriptions of some popular party games. Do you know what they are?

578 A curly-tailed animal is requested to make the sound of a mouse.

579 A search is undertaken for a finger protector.

580 Upon the cessation of harmonic cadences all but one may find a seat.

581 All participants encircle an agriculturalist in his retreat.

582 Everyone flees as a pursuer tries to find a recipient for an amorous gesture.

583 A murmured message travels orientally.

584 The letters on this board contain the names of eighteen card or board games. They can be found horizontally, diagonally, vertically or backwards.

N	E	R	I	A	T	I	L	O	S
O	D	U	L	O	T	T	O	E	Y
M	R	O	T	S	I	H	W	L	L
M	A	Y	M	M	U	R	F	B	O
A	U	M	A	I	D	E	I	B	P
G	G	D	L	O	N	K	S	A	O
K	H	B	I	N	G	O	H	R	N
C	T	A	E	H	C	P	E	C	O
A	S	R	I	A	P	A	N	S	M
B	T	E	K	R	A	M	W	E	N

AUGUST

Dog days

The dog days are the hottest days of the summer. Sirius, the dog-star, is the brightest in the sky and during July and August it rises and sets with the sun. The Romans believed that it helped to make the weather extra warm! Another superstition is that this star, in the constellation of Canis Major, the Great Dog, has a direct influence over the canine species!

What . . .

585 is the name of the world-famous dog show, held in London?
586 is a 'toy' dog?
587 is 'docking' a dog's tail?
588 is the Kennel Club?
589 person has the catch word 'walkies!'?
590 does the owner of every dog in Britain over the age of six months require by law?

Which dog . . .

591 sits listening to His Master's Voice?
592 belongs to Mr Punch?
593 was the Darling family's pet?
594 guarded his master's grave in Scotland for many years?
595 led a cat and a bull-terrier on an incredible journey?
596 might be found near a magic roundabout?
597 is a beagle with a cute line in comment?
598 belonged to Dorothy?
599 led his wife and ninety-seven dalmatian puppies from Suffolk to Regent's Park?

What ...

600 are bloodhounds noted for?

601 were pointers originally bred for?

602 do bitzers and mutts have in common?

603 person's 'eyes' might have a cold nose?

604 might a clergyman do with a dog-collar?

605 is the smallest recognized breed of dog in the world?

606 open-air competitions test teams of dogs and handlers on their ability to herd and pen sheep?

607 strange characteristic does the basenji have?

608 is the wild dog of Australia?

609 What sorts of dog are these and where did they originally come from? If you know you should be able to match them to their dotty dog food!

On your travels

You may be off on your travels this month. Whether you are going by Rolls Royce, rickshaw or roller skates, see if you can answer these questions and be transported with delight!

Who ...

610 went to sea in a sieve?

611 was told that she'd 'look sweet upon the seat of a bicycle made for two'?

612 often travelled through the jungle with Jane, swinging from the trees?

613 sailed in an ark with his family and lots of animals?

614 travels through space and time in a police telephone box?

615 had an extraordinary Aston Martin made for him by 'Q'?

616 often used her umbrella as a means of transport?

What form of transport is or was ...

617 the Brighton Belle?

618 the Flying Hamburger?

619 a Sopwith Camel?

620 a Graf Zeppelin?

621 Chitty Chitty Bang Bang?

622 the Spirit of St Louis?

623 a penny-farthing?

Which ...

624 train hauled coal and earned its nickname because it puffed out so much smoke?

625 car was mass produced by Henry Ford and could be bought in any colour 'as long as it was black'?

626 ship, sunk in the reign of Henry VIII, was raised from the Solent in 1982?

627 supersonic passenger aircraft was produced jointly by England and France?

What came first ...

628 sedan chairs or rickshaws?
629 Liverpool Street station or Paddington station?
630 jet-propelled aeroplanes or the Royal Air Force?
631 the launching of the *Queen Elizabeth II* or the sinking of *Queen Elizabeth I* in Hong Kong harbour?

632 Can you find the correct home for these means of transport?

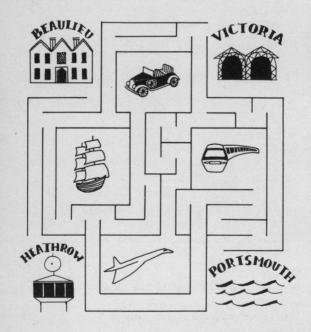

Picnic posers

When the weather is fine it's not only teddy bears who enjoy picnics! Food is supposed to taste better out of doors, so pack up your vacuum flask and sandwiches and be sure to take this quiz with you.

Who ...

633 dared to ask for more?

634 told a story about a treacle well at the Mad Hatter's tea party?

635 'dined on mince and slices of quince'?

636 was the frog who served his guests roasted grasshopper in ladybird sauce?

637 obtains his great strength from eating spinach?

638 lived at Kanga's and had extract of malt for breakfast, dinner and tea?

639 expired as a result of 'chewing little bits of string'?

640 had a 'Wonka's Whipple Scrumptious Fudge Mallow Delight'?

Which or what ...

641 snack was invented by an earl who did not want to get his playing cards dirty?

642 sort of food is associated with Clarence Birdseye?

643 gentleman is associated with 57 Varieties?

644 name is given to cooking out of doors over charcoal?

645 popular drink originated in China in 2000 B.C.?

646 is produced by bees and spread on bread?

647 is black pudding?

648 bean can be processed to resemble meat?

What do these have in common?

649 Horseradish, cranberry and soy.

650 Plait, bloomer and cottage.

651 Mayonnaise, meringue and omelettes.

652 Moussaka, baklava and pitta bread.
653 Basil, thyme and bay.
654 Sieve, colander and tea-strainer.
655 Mashed, duchesse and chipped.
656 Mulligatawny, cock-a-leekie and vichyssoise.

657 Can you identify these foods?

August Bank Holiday

No school, the sun's shining and you might be going to the beach this month. So pack your swimming costume, grab your bucket and spade and dig in! 'Oh, I do love to be beside the sea-side ...'

Name ...
658 the resort with a tower overlooking a golden mile.
659 a conqueror's battle base which became a Cinque Port.
660 the location of the peerless pier.

661 the port described in song as having bluebirds flying over its white cliffs.

662 the town whose pirates Gilbert and Sullivan wrote about.

663 the fishing town, noted for jet, that has an ancient ruined abbey.

664 What is this angler fishing for?

Come on in – the water's lovely!

665 What headless creature has feet growing from its arms?

666 How many legs do crabs, prawns and shrimps all have?

667 Why do lobsters shed their shells?

668 What precious 'stone' might be found in an oyster?

669 Are sea-anemones plants or animals?

670 What aggressive Iberian is made of 'jelly'?

Flotsam and jetsam:

671   Who did the carpenter eat oysters with?

672   What is the largest sea-bird ...

673   ... and who shot one and lived to regret it?

674   What is a mermaid's purse?

675   Which magic dragon lived by the sea?

676   Who is often to hand on the beach with his long-suffering wife and dog Toby?

677   When you've said 'She sells sea-shells on the sea-shore' six times quickly without a mistake, try and identify the shells she sells! When you've done it, rearrange the boxed letters to find the family name of the group.

SEPTEMBER

The first day of term

A new teacher, a new class or a new school are all possibilities this month. How well informed are you about education? Do this quiz and you may end up knowing more about it than your teacher!

678 At what age are British children required by law to start their education?
679 In what year did free secondary education become available for all children?
680 What is the present minimum school-leaving age?
681 What do the letters G.C.E. stand for?
682 Are any school subjects compulsory?

What ...
683 sort of trade would an apprentice learn from a master cooper?
684 schools gave children the chance to learn reading, writing and religion once a week?
685 method of teaching was used in monitorial schools?
686 famous public school near Windsor was founded by Henry VI?
687 sport, according to tradition, was invented at a school of the same name?
688 is Oxbridge?
689 career would you have in mind if you went to (a) Norlands; (b) Sandhurst; (c) White Lodge?

What . . .

690 were hornbooks?

691 are known as the three Rs?

692 is a curriculum?

693 age did you have to be in order to leave school in 1950?

694 form of technology composed of software and hardware might be found in a school?

695 Complete these playground sayings: (a) A pinch and a punch . . . (b) Knock, knock . . . (c) Finders keepers . . .

696 What is this teacher trying to tell his class about their schooldays? You may not agree with him!

Harvest

This is the time of year for the Harvest Festival, a thanksgiving for successful harvests. Some schools ask children to bring in food to be displayed and then distributed to the needy people in the area. Can you answer these questions about common foods?

Bread:

697 What is usually added to dough to make it rise?
698 What grain is most commonly used to make white bread?
699 At what meal did the King want 'some butter for the Royal slice of bread'?
700 What is unleavened bread?
701 With which countries are these breads associated:
(a) pitta; (b) nan; (c) pumpernickel?

Salt:

702 Which word, meaning 'earnings', is derived from an allowance of salt?
703 What is brine?
704 Which sea is so salty that it can support no life?
705 Who in the Bible was turned into a pillar of salt?
706 Who might be referred to as an 'old salt'?

Tea:

707 What stimulant does tea contain?
708 Which country is noted for its tea ceremonies?
709 What is a samovar?
710 Which leaves are picked for the best tea?
711 Who tried to put a dormouse into a teapot?

Rice:

712 What name is given to the fields in which rice is grown?
713 When might you have dried rice thrown at you?
714 Why is rice such an important crop?
715 What is brown rice?
716 With which countries are these rice dishes associated:
(a) paella; (b) risotto; (c) biryani?

Sugar:

717 Is the most sugar obtained from the stem, leaf or root of a plant?

718 According to the rhyme, what are little girls made of?
719 What happens when sugar is heated to 200° centigrade?
720 What are molasses?
721 Which is finest: (a) caster; (b) icing; (c) granulated sugar?

Cheese:
722 What is known as the 'king of cheeses'?
723 What are curds and whey?
724 Why do photographers often ask you to say 'cheese'?
725 With which countries are these cheeses associated: (a) gruyère; (b) edam; (c) feta?
726 Which cheese has the least amount of fat per ounce: (a) cheddar; (b) cottage cheese; (c) cream cheese?

The last night of the Proms

Sir Henry Wood began the Promenade Concerts in 1895 at the Queen's Hall. When the building was destroyed in 1941 they continued at the Royal Albert Hall where they are held to this day. At a 'Prom' some of the audience stand in an open area of the concert hall where they are allowed to promenade or walk about if there's room, which is most unlikely at the popular last night!

What ...

727 are the four sections of an orchestra?

728 is 'playing by ear'?

729 is a steel band?

730 is chamber music?

731 number of records must be sold to get a gold disc?

732 are madrigals?

733 is a staff?

734 is a score?

Who ...

735 is the leader of the orchestra?

736 was a child prodigy and composed many operas including *The Magic Flute*?

737 lifted spirits with her singing during the Second World War and was known as the Forces' Sweetheart?

738 wrote nine symphonies, but went deaf and had to 'hear' his final works in his head?

739 was the most famous violin-maker of all time?

740 played the violin so fast that people said he was in league with the devil?

741 gyrated his pelvis while he sang and became known as 'The King'?

742 gave his audience a surprise in a symphony?

What do these have in common?

743 'Eroica', 'Pastoral' and 'Choral'.

744 Tabor, kazoo and hurdy-gurdy.

745 La Scala, Glyndebourne and Covent Garden.

746 Herbert von Karajan, Sir Malcolm Sargent and Simon Rattle.

747 'Michelle', 'Yesterday' and 'Penny Lane'.

748 Double bass, tuba and double bassoon.

749 Kiri Te Kanawa, Maria Callas and Joan Sutherland.

750 *Jesus Christ Superstar*, *Evita* and *Joseph and the Amazing Technicolour Dreamcoat*.

751 Larry Adler, Louis Armstrong, Jacqueline du Pré, Andrés Segovia, James Galway and Kyung Wha Chung are (or were) virtuosos. Which musical instrument is each person connected with?

Battle of Britain Day: 15 September

Adolf Hitler knew that any plan to invade the British Isles must involve the destruction of Britain's air power. From 12 August to 17 September 1940 British airmen fought off the threat of the German Luftwaffe until Hitler was forced to postpone his plans. History is full of such bravery, so do battle with these questions and see if you emerge victorious!

In which battle ...

752 in 1066 did King Harold die?

753 in 1485 was the first Tudor king victorious?

754 in 1571 were galleys used for the last time for fighting at sea?

755 in 1805 did the British fleet do its duty and live up to the nation's expectations?

756 in 1836 were Davy Crockett and 200 Texans killed?

757 in 1863 were the Confederates under Robert E. Lee defeated?

758 in 1916 were tanks used in battle for the first time?

What name is given to ...

759 Japanese professional warriors who fought with long-bows and swords?

760 Christian soldiers whose aim was to drive Muslims from the Holy Land?

761 regiments of Nepalese soldiers who serve in the British army?

762 the nomadic people who conquered northern China under Genghis Khan?

763 small bodies of fighters who act independently and take their name from the Spanish for 'little war'?

764 the Japanese pilots who deliberately crashed their planes on targets in the Second World War?

Which ...

765 admiral said, 'I have only one eye. I have a right to be blind sometimes'?

766 queen of the Iceni led her people in a rebellion against the Romans?

767 two fat little men agreed to have a battle over the spoiling of a rattle?

768 French woman led an army to defeat the English at Orleans and was later burnt at the stake?

769 statesman declared, 'We shall fight on the beaches'?

770 grave in Westminster Abbey serves as a memorial to those killed in both World Wars?

771 Duke is supposed to have said that the Battle of Waterloo was won on the playing fields of Eton?

772 Who fought against whom?

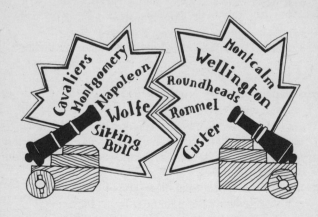

Cavaliers   Montgomery   Napoleon   Wolfe   Sitting Bull

Montcalm   Wellington   Roundheads   Rommel   Custer

OCTOBER

Winnie-the-Pooh's birthday: *14 October*

Winnie-the-Pooh was first published on 14 October 1926 and Pooh has become famous for his hums, love of honey and the odd situations he gets into. See what bear facts you know!

Which bear ...

773 has 'very little brain'?

774 came from Peru via a London station?

775 taught Mowgli the law of the jungle?

776 has a frog for a friend?

777 wears yellow checked trousers?

778 has a canine friend called Sweep?

779 lives in Jellystone Park and is 'smarter than the average bear'?

780 belongs to Deborah Robinson?

Do you know ...

781 which bear's diet consists mostly of seals?

782 why polar bears have hair on the soles of their feet?

783 the name of the only type of bear native to the southern hemisphere?

784 the name of the smallest type of bear?

785 which bear's Latin name is Ursus Horribilis?

786 when and where bear cubs are usually born?

787 which bear-like animal is the symbol of the World Wildlife Fund?

788 which 'bear' is really a marsupial?

Which or what ...

789 bears live in the night sky?

790 Tennessee gentleman, according to the song, 'killed him a bear when he was only three'?

791 American President was closely associated with bears?

792 do Bernie Winters, Orson Welles and Ursula Andress have in common?

793 European country's capital is said to be named after a bear?

794 Shakespearian play has the stage direction, 'Exit, pursued by a bear'?

795 happened in a bear garden?

796 City institution may contain bears or bulls in men's clothing?

797 Who's coming to tea
   Just to see me?
   We'll start on the eating
   When you know the greeting!

An adventure quiz: *22 October*

On 22 October 1978 Prince Charles officially launched
Operation Drake at Plymouth. It was designed to give young
people the chance to 'reawaken and commemorate the old
Elizabethan spirit of challenge and adventure' as they followed
Drake's progress around the world in their ship, the *Eye of the
Wind*.

How brave are you feeling? First you must identify some
famous adventurers and then plunge in among the sharks to
find the names of some fictional heroes. A few final clues
and you reach the safety of home.

798 I am a lighthouse-keeper's daughter. In 1838 we rowed
     out in a fierce storm to save the crew of a wrecked
     ship.

799 My first names are Thomas Edward but my association
     with the Arabs gave me a different name. I helped them
     in their fight against the Turks and led them into
     Damascus in 1918.

800 I was the first man to sail around the world single-
     handed, in my boat *Gypsy Moth IV*. I was knighted
     with Sir Francis Drake's sword.

801 I established several long-distance flying records, includ-
     ing England to Australia in 1930.

802 I led two expeditions to the Antarctic and reached the
     South Pole on the second one only to find that someone
     had got there first.

803 I visited the court of the Kublai Khan with my father
     and uncle and spent some years in the service of the
     emperor. I later wrote about my travels while in prison.

804 I am a British travel writer. I began my career in the
     Arab countries in the 1920s and enjoyed travelling well
     into my eighties.

805 I charted the coast of New Zealand, navigated the Great
     Barrier Reef and explored the Antarctic.

806 Rescue the fictional adventurers by claiming their missing letters from the vowel-eating shark. You will find a pilot, a knight, a castaway, a sailor, an apeman, a tale-teller and a couple of superheroes!

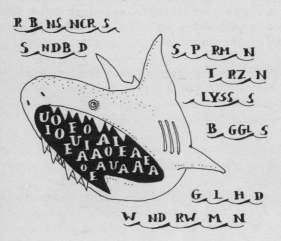

R B NS NCR S

S NDB D

S P RM N

T RZ N

LYSS S

B GGL S

G L H D

W ND RW M N

UO IOFO EUIAI EAAOEAE OEAUAAA

How many . . .

807 men are left clinging to the wreckage at the end of the film *Jaws*?

808 times can you live, according to the title of a James Bond film?

809 musketeers did Dumas originally create?

810 Now name the island which won the George Cross for its heroic resistance in the Second World War and you are home!

United Nations Day: *24 October*

The United Nations was founded on the 24 October 1945 to tackle the problems of poverty, prejudice and inequality. Finding out how other people live and what they believe in is the first step towards this. What do you know about the peoples of the world?

What countries do you associate with these people?
811 Walloons.
812 Apaches.
813 Aborigines.
814 Maoris.
815 Cossacks.

In which religion ...
816 is a pilgrimage to Mecca the ambition of the faithful?
817 do boys come of age at a ceremony called Barmitzvah?
818 is the supreme god known as Brahman?
819 are you christened?
820 do all men have the name Singh as well as their family name?

In which countries are these newspapers published?
821 *Le Monde.*
822 *Die Welt.*
823 The *Observer.*
824 *Wall Street Journal.*
825 *La Stampa.*

Link the purchase to the payment:
826 Ticket for a bull-fight.
827 Worry beads.
828 An ice-cream in Disneyland.
829 A ride on a gondola.
830 A sari.

lira
pesetas
drachmas
rupees
dollars

Can you identify these Nobel Peace Prize winners?

831   1952. A doctor who founded a hospital in Africa to fight leprosy.

832   1978. Egyptian and Israeli statesmen who met to try and find a peaceful solution to their countries' problems.

833   1964. American Civil Rights leader who believed in a policy of non-violence and was assassinated.

834   1979. Yugoslavian nun who founded an order of missionaries in Calcutta to care for the sick.

835   Sort out the symbol! Each answer is a five-letter word. Start from the centre. The first one has been done for you. If you answer correctly, the first letters plus the centre O can be rearranged to name an international language.

(a)   A country noted for its pyramids.

(b)   Part of the Iberian peninsula.

(c)   Home of the Eiffel Tower.

(d)   Chief river of Western Europe.

(e)   Kingdom in South-East Asia with a capital called Katmandu.

(f)   Capital of Japan.

(g)   Swiss mountain with a dangerous north face.

(h)   Long South American mountain range.

Hallowe'en: *31 October*

The spookiest night of the year! Spectres and spirits may waft around and your knees may be knocking, but don't give up the ghost – get on with this eerie quiz!

Which witch ...

836 lived in a gingerbread house?
837 had a servant called Dulboot?
838 had a cat called Mog?
839 gave Edmund Pevensie Turkish delight?
840 could not resist giving the bedknob a little twist?

Which wizard ...

841 of Earthsea unloosed a 'shadow beast'?
842 went to tea with a hobbit?
843 was originally a balloonist from Omaha?
844 befriended a boy called Carrot 900 years out of his own time?
845 is said to have made the Round Table?

Which fairy ...

846 danced in *The Nutcracker*?
847 loved Bottom?
848 gave Princess Amy the gift of ordinariness?
849 drank poison to save Peter Pan?
850 had a sister called Mrs Bedonebyasyoudid?

Which ghost ...

851 is said to run along the 'haunted gallery' at Hampton Court?
852 sat in Macbeth's chair at a banquet?
853 first appeared to Scrooge on a doorknocker?
854 is said to lead other vessels to destruction around the Cape of Good Hope?
855 helps people to write their books?

Which . . .

856 saints' day follows Hallowe'en?

857 New England town is particularly associated with witchcraft?

858 options are given by American children as they go from house to house on Hallowe'en?

859 Jack is said to lead travellers astray?

860 vegetables are associated with Hallowe'en?

861 Can you work out the three magic sayings in the cauldron?

NOVEMBER

Guy Fawkes' night: *5 November*

If Guy Fawkes had succeeded in blowing up the Houses of
Parliament in 1605 the results would have been disastrous.
He has remained a favourite 'baddie' ever since. This quiz
is about well-known baddies and explosive situations –
strictly for bright sparks with strong nerves!

Which or what ...

862 emperor was said to have fiddled while Rome burnt?
863 Californian city was devastated by an earthquake and
a three-day fire in 1906?
864 Italian city was buried under volcanic ash from Vesuvius
in A.D. 7?
865 lane was the site of the start of the fire of London?
866 British airship was destroyed by fire in 1930 in France?
867 age must you be before you can purchase fireworks?
868 explosive was discovered by Alfred Nobel?
869 is the abbreviation by which trinitrotoluene is generally
known?
870 are pyrotechnics?
871 saint gave her name to a circular firework?
872 mythological bird rose from the ashes of its own funeral
pyre?
873 colour fireworks are produced when these salts are
added: (a) copper; (b) sodium; (c) barium?

Can you identify these characters? They all share bad reputations!

874 A Chicago gangster eventually imprisoned for income tax evasion.

875 A beautiful woman who discovered the secret of Samson's strength and betrayed him.

876 A king thought to have been responsible for the murder of two little princes in the Tower of London.

877 A king of the Huns, known as the 'Scourge of God'.

878 A notorious American outlaw who specialized in bank hold-ups and initiated the art of train robbery.

879 An Austrian-born leader of the Nazi party who died in a bunker?

880 Some fictional baddies have signed their names and left some graffiti in the cellar. They have changed the letters around to hide their identities – but you will be able to find them, won't you?

The Lord Mayor's Show

A Lord Mayor of London has been elected every year since 1192. On the second Saturday in November his or her election is celebrated with a procession from Guildhall to the Law Courts in the Strand with floats and pageantry representing various City companies. How much do you know about London?

Which ...

881 ancient monument once stood in Egypt and now stands by the Thames?

882 column in London is 61.5 metres tall, and why?

883 square contains the statue of a man three times larger than life?

884 church contains the Coronation Chair?

885 building contains the epitaph to its architect, 'If you would see his monument, look around'?

886 park contains the statue of the little boy who didn't want to grow up?

887 museum is noted for its skeletons of dinosaurs?

888 tower contains a bell named after Sir Benjamin Hall?

Who lives or lived at ...

889 Apsley House, Hyde Park Corner, and became known as the 'Iron Duke'?

890 221B Baker Street and found solving crimes 'elementary'?

891 11 Downing Street and has to budget carefully?

892 the Mansion House for a year and may or may not return?

893 48 Doughty Street and created, amongst others, Oliver, Nicholas, David and Little Nell?

894 17 Gough Square, wrote a famous dictionary and is buried standing up in Westminster Abbey?

895 12 Buckingham Street and kept a famous diary?

896 10 South Street and became known as the 'lady with the lamp'?

What ...

897 Londoners are traditionally born within the sound of Bow Bells?

898 did the bells of London tell Dick Whittington to do?

899 ceremony takes place nightly in the Tower of London?

900 is known as the 'street of ink'?

901 church's bells rang the peal of 'oranges and lemons'?

902 is the 'Old Lady of Threadneedle Street' otherwise known as?

903 West Indian celebration is held annually in West London?

904 part of London is referred to as the 'square mile'?

905 Can you put the bridges in the correct order across the Thames? The names are: Southwark, Waterloo, Tower, Blackfriars, Westminster and London.

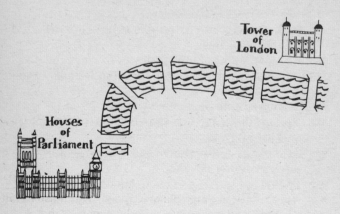

The State Opening of Parliament

Every year the three elements that make up Parliament come together – the Commons, the Lords and the Sovereign. The Queen's speech is written by her ministers and outlines their plans for the next session. It is only after this has been read that a new session of Parliament can begin. Now is your chance to find out how well informed you are.

Choose the correct answer to the following questions:

906 Who or what is Black Rod?
  (a) A rare plant that grows in Westminster.
  (b) The official who summons the Commons to the Lords.
  (c) The line that separates the Government from the Opposition.

907 The Strangers' Gallery is ...
  (a) the place from which the public may view debates in the Commons
  (b) a missing persons bureau
  (c) a room in Westminster where portraits of famous visitors are hung.

908 Lobbying your M.P. means ...
  (a) throwing eggs and other missiles to get his attention
  (b) asking him to visit your home
  (c) going to Westminster to persuade your M.P. to see your point of view.

909 Hansard ...
  (a) was the architect who designed Westminster Hall
  (b) is the official report of Parliamentary debates
  (c) is a special drink only available in the House of Commons.

910 The first woman to sit in the House of Commons
was ...
   (a) Lady Astor
   (b) Emily Pankhurst
   (c) Barbara Castle.

911 A maiden speech is ...
   (a) a speech made by a woman
   (b) an M.P.'s first speech in Parliament
   (c) a speech about the rights of women.

912 When an M.P. wishes to retire he applies for ...
   (a) stewardship of the Chiltern Hundreds
   (b) a place in the House of Lords
   (c) the position of Lord Mayor.

913 Voting is compulsory in ...
   (a) England
   (b) France
   (c) Australia.

914 Can you link the quotations to the politicians who
uttered them?

1 MOST OF OUR PEOPLE HAVE NEVER HAD IT SO GOOD.

2 I HAVE NOTHING TO OFFER BUT BLOOD, TOIL, TEARS AND SWEAT.

3 THE LADY'S NOT FOR TURNING.

4 THOUGH I SIT DOWN NOW, THE TIME WILL COME WHEN YOU WILL HEAR ME SPEAK.

5 I BELIEVE IT IS PEACE FOR OUR TIME.

St Andrew's Day: *30 November*

St Andrew is the patron saint of Scotland and tradition says that his remains were brought to Fife in A.D. 368. He was a fisherman and the brother of St Peter.

Whether you take the high road or the low road to Scotland, there's plenty to see north of the border.

What am I?

915 A kind of prickly plant and my country's heraldic emblem.
916 A humble creature who taught perseverance to a king.
917 I am said to be haunted, I was the scene of Duncan's murder at the hand of Macbeth and I was the birth-place of Princess Margaret.
918 I am a kind of material hand-made in the Outer Hebrides.
919 A pouch, usually covered with fur and worn hanging from the waist.
920 A royal holiday home, purchased by Prince Albert.
921 A celebration on 25 January of the birth of a famous poet.
922 A dish made from minced heart, lungs and liver, oat-meal, suet and spices and cooked in a stomach.

True or False?

923 The Flying Scotsman is a Scottish Superman.
924 Marmalade was first made in Dundee.
925 Bagpipes are made from cows' udders.
926 J. M. Barrie, Robert Louis Stevenson and David Living-stone were all Scottish.
927 The bones of Sir John Napier were used for counting.
928 Tam o' Shanter is a type of hat.
929 Arbroath smokies are Scottish cigars.
930 A Highland fling is a long throw of the hammer in the famous Scottish sport of 'tossing the hammer'.

First answer all the questions,
Then put in order on their own
The first letters of each word,
And you will find the monster's home!

931 Famous for a festival, a fringe and a tattoo.
932 A royal palace in Edinburgh, named after a cross.
933 Islands about eight miles to the north of Scotland, across the Pentland Firth.
934 The largest Scottish loch.
935 The author of *Rob Roy*, *Lord of the Isles* and the *Lady of the Lake*.
936 A big Ben!
937 A roughly trimmed trunk to be tossed.
938 Bonnie Prince Charlie fled here 'over the sea'.

DECEMBER

All friends together

School holidays give you a chance to spend more time with your friends. This quiz is about famous partners and friends. You can compete with a friend to see who can score more points or, if you are feeling really friendly, try doing it together!

Who ...

939 was Cinderella's faithful friend?
940 asked his friend Hardy to kiss him before he died?
941 went to tell the King that the sky was falling down and collected all his friends along the way?
942 is Batman's adventurous friend?
943 is Noddy's Toytown friend?
944 is See-Threepio's robot friend?
945 was Butch Cassidy's friend and partner in crime?
946 helps Yogi Bear when he is in trouble with the Ranger?

Here are some famous people. Can you name their partners and what they did together?

947 Gilbert	*Sergeant Pepper*	Bailey
948 Rolls	*The Mikado*	Allen
949 Barnum	'Underneath the Arches'	Lloyd Webber
950 Lennon	Non-stop Atlantic flight	Sullivan
951 Rice	engines	Spencer
952 Flanagan	ice-skating	Brown
953 Woodward	'The Greatest Show on Earth'	
		Royce
954 Alcock	St Michael	McCartney
955 Torvill	*Evita*	Bernstein
956 Marks	Watergate	Dean

957 Hide and seek: can you find all the people in this picture?

The longest night of the year: *22 December*

The night of the winter solstice, usually 22 December, is the longest night of the year in the Northern hemisphere because the sun is then at its furthest point from the equator. You'll have plenty of time to gaze into space, so if it's a clear night you'll be able to see the stars and who knows what else . . .

What . . .

958 name is given to the explosion which some people believe marked the origin of the universe?

959 do we call a region in space where gravity is so strong that not even light can escape its pull?

960 is the Milky Way?
961 happens during a total eclipse of the sun?
962 American space programme aimed to place men on the moon by 1970?
963 is launched like a rocket and lands on a runway?
964 is a light year?
965 was special about the handshake between commanders Leonov and Stafford in July 1975?
966 is the difference between a planet and a star?

Which planet ...

967 is closest to the sun?
968 rotates on its axis from east to west?
969 is largely covered by water and has one moon?
970 is named after the Roman god of war and is sometimes called the red planet?
971 is larger than all the other planets in our solar system put together and has a big red spot?
972 has spectacular rings and is the second largest planet in the solar system?
973 was the first to be discovered by telescope in 1781 by Sir William Herschel?
974 has two satellites, Nereid and Triton, and takes about 165 years to orbit the sun?
975 is the outermost of the known planets?

Who ...

976 was the second man to step onto the moon?
977 is Luke Skywalker's twin sister?
978 was a doctor who travelled in space and time?
979 wrote about a Martian invasion in the *War of the Worlds*?
980 jumped over the moon?
981 wrote a suite of music called 'The Planets'?
982 was the first man in space?
983 was the first woman in space?

984 developed the theory of gravity and realized that it was the force that keeps the planets in their orbits round the sun?

985 gave his name to a famous comet which is due to become visible from Earth again in 1986?

See how quickly you can travel through the maze from Earth to Planet Xenon but beware of the dreaded Space Blasters with their all-seeing eyes who are lying in wait to trap unwary spacemen!

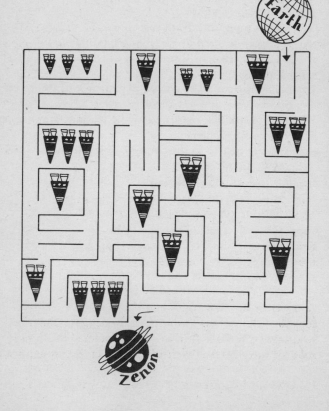

A *family party*

This is the time of year when families get together. Make your party go with a swing by getting everybody to join in this quiz. You will find out just how familiar your family is with other families!

What relation ...

986 was Richard I to King John?
987 was Icarus to Daedalus?
988 is Lisa Minnelli to Judy Garland?
989 is Topsy to Tim?
990 was Mary, Queen of Scots, to Queen Elizabeth I?
991 would your sisterless uncle's only brother's son be to your mother?
992 is Prince William to Princess Anne?
993 were the ugly sisters to Cinderella?

The following people belong to famous families. Who are they?

994 Meg, Jo, Beth and Amy.
995 Groucho, Harpo, Zeppo and Chico.
996 Shem, Ham and Japheth.
997 Bridget, Roger, Titty, John and Susan.
998 Wendy, John and Michael.
999 Henry, Jane and Peter.
1000 Charles, Anne, Edward and Andrew.
1001 Pod, Homily and Arrietty.

What ...

1002 street do the Ruggles family live in?
1003 little house was the home of the Ingalls family?
1004 card game is associated with contented relations?
1005 country did the Pevensey children enter through a wardrobe?
1006 happened to the father of the 'railway children'?

1007   war made life dangerous for the 'children of the New
       Forest'?

1008   city did Romulus and Remus traditionally found?

1009   Finnish family live in a valley and have Trolls for
       ancestors?

1010   This 'family tree' is made up of some famous sisters.
       Who are they?
       (a)   They lived in Yorkshire and wrote many books.
       (b)   Five sisters who sing for their supper.
       (c)   Two American film stars who haven't spoken to
             each other for years.
       (d)   Two public figures with royal connections.
       (e)   A television star from a soap opera and a writer.
       (f)   Two girls from Glasgow who sing and dance.
       (g)   Five sisters who were glittering débutantes and lived
             in a 'cold climate'.

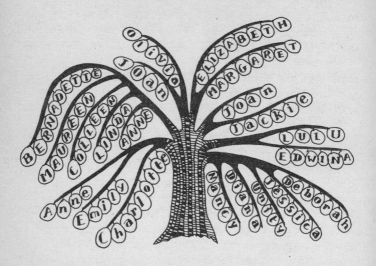

Christmas Day: *25 December*

Christmas has been observed in England for centuries. The actual date of Jesus's birth has never been known and until the fifth century Christmas was celebrated on all sorts of days. The early Christians probably decided on 25 December as it's very near the winter solstice, which was an important date in the pagan calendar, being the festival of the Great Yule Feast. It is supposed to be a time of good cheer, so if you don't know all the answers to this quiz, just grin and bear it!

On Christmas Day:

1011 In 1932 what was broadcast for the first time?

1012 What did my true love give to me?

1013 According to the carol, how many ships went sailing by?

1014 In 1950 the Stone of Scone was stolen. What is it, and where was it stolen from?

1015 Which Dickensian character cried, 'God bless us, every one!'?

1016 Which character created by Raymond Briggs declared, 'Happy blooming Christmas to you, too!'?

1017 What did Little Jack Horner pull out of the Christmas pie?

1018 Crack the quizzical candles on the Christmas card and discover a greeting in the process:

(a)   Something to wear that you get from a cracker.

(b)   They appeared to shepherds with glad tidings.

(c)   Fruity Christmas dessert.

(d)   A tree to find a partridge in.

(e)   An old-fashioned name for the Christmas season.

(f)   Seasonal songs.

(g)   Festive greenery with red berries.

(h)   Reindeer with a shiny nose.

(i)   Mary and Joseph found no room at this place.

(j)   The Three Kings followed one.

(k)   A Christmas gift from the people of Oslo to London.

(l)   Plant above a Christmas kiss.

(m)   A special calendar opened in December.

(n)   You might hang one up for Santa to fill!

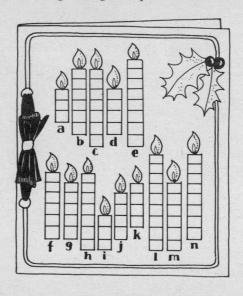

ANSWERS

1 6 January. There are twelve days to Christmas and it is supposed to be unlucky to leave decorations up after this date.

2 29 February, in a Leap Year, is traditionally a day when women may propose marriage!

3 Mothering Sunday is celebrated in mid-Lent; it's for making the most of your mum.

4 Her Majesty the Queen was born on 21 April. She also has an official birthday in June, celebrated by Trooping the Colour.

5 The F.A. Cup. The final is played at Wembley.

6 The Wimbledon tennis tournament is traditionally associated with June. Love (no score) will definitely not win the match!

7 Swan Upping, the practice of marking swans for future identification by nicking their beaks.

8 The grouse-shooting season.

9 Michaelmas Day is 29 September, which is one of the quarter days. Michaelmas daisies also flower at this time.

10 Trafalgar Day commemorates Lord Nelson's victory over the French in 1805.

11 The Veteran Car Run from London to Brighton.

12 St Nicholas' Day – 6 December.

13 Help with the washing up.

14 First born.

15 First night.

16 First Aid.

17 First Lady.

18 First-foot.

19 Be nice to brother Ben.

20 Catseyes. Percy Shaw was saved from driving off the edge of the road in thick fog when he saw a cat's eyes gleam in the dark. Experimenting with glass set in rubber and iron, he designed a stud to reflect light from cars' headlamps and called his invention 'catseyes'. They were first used in 1934.

21 The mackintosh. This was named after Charles Macintosh, who invented a waterproof fabric using rubber, which was patented in 1823.

22 Television. The first set was called a televisor and was made from a cardboard disc with glass around it, parts of old radios, electric motors and other bits and pieces. Baird demonstrated his invention to the Royal Institution for Scientific Research in 1926.

23 The flushing water closet or W.C. Some ancient civilizations had toilets, but by the Middle Ages people seemed to have forgotten how to make drains and flushing systems. In the sixteenth century Sir John Harington invented a flush lavatory and his godmother, Elizabeth I, ordered one for herself at Richmond Palace.

24 The Hovercraft. In 1954 Christopher Cockerell set up his cans and scales, an experiment that led to his hovercraft design. The first cross-Channel passenger and car ferry service in hovercrafts began in 1968.

25 Turn out the toy cupboard.

26 F, S (days of the week).

27 Callaghan, Thatcher (Prime Ministers).

28 50, 100 (British coins).

29 XL, L (Roman numerals).

30 Aries, Taurus (signs of the zodiac).

31 Try harder at school.

32 Neil Armstrong, on 21 July 1969. He declared, 'That's one small step for a man, one giant leap for mankind.'

33 Margaret Thatcher. She became an M.P. in 1959, was elected Leader of the Conservative Party in 1975 and became Prime Minister in 1979.

34 Charles Blondin. He first achieved this feat in 1859 and repeated it many times in many ways. Once he sat down in the middle and made an omelette!

35 Roger Bannister. His time, in 1954, was 3 minutes, 59.4 seconds.

36 Dr Sally Ride. From 19 to 24 June 1983, Dr Ride and four male colleagues flew on the American space shuttle.

37 I won't blot my copybook.

38 Rip Van Winkle in the story by Washington Irving.

39 Sleeping Beauty.

40 Little Boy Blue.

41 The Princess in the story of 'The Princess and the Pea' by Hans Andersen. The test of a true princess involved the placing of a pea under her mattress. Only a real princess would be able to feel it!

42 Goldilocks. She found Baby Bear's bed to be the most comfortable.

43 The Giant in 'Jack and the Beanstalk'.

44 Gulliver in *Gulliver's Travels* by Jonathan Swift.

45 Alice in *Alice in Wonderland* by Lewis Carroll.

46 Max in *Where the Wild Things Are* by Maurice Sendak.

47 The wicked wolf in 'Little Red Riding Hood'.

48 Sleepy.

49 Joseph, in the musical written by Tim Rice and Andrew Lloyd Webber, based on the Bible story.

50 Wee Willie Winkie.

51 Bing Crosby in the song that broke records for its popularity.

52 The tsetse fly from Africa.

53 Sleepwalks.

54 A local anaesthetic affects one area of the body; a general anaesthetic sends the whole mind and body to sleep.

55 An insomniac.

56 A dormouse.

57 'Rock-a-bye-baby on the tree top'.

58 To send someone into a sleeplike state when they will normally do anything that is suggested to them.

59 The beds in the picture are: a four poster; a cradle; a sleeping bag; bunk beds; a hammock.

60 Ayers Rock, in the Central Desert of Australia. It is famous for its colour changes.

61 The Great Barrier Reef, made of coral; it is the largest reef in the world.

62 Gold was discovered by Edward Hargreaves at Bathurst, New South Wales. People flocked there, hoping to find some for themselves.

63 Sydney. It has a huge natural harbour and an opera house with a roof designed to look like the sails of a yacht.

64 Outback or bush.

65 The koala bear. It is a marsupial.

66 The kookaburra, which has a call like mocking laughter.

67 The kangaroo. The kangaroo family also includes smaller animals like wallabies.

68 The duck-billed platypus, an amphibious animal.

69 The emu, which is similar to an ostrich. Its wings are undeveloped but it can run quite fast.

70 The Aborigines.

71 The School of the Air. Lessons are given over two-way radio. You would probably only meet the rest of your class once a year at a summer camp.

72 The Flying Doctor, a service founded by the Reverend John Flynn in 1928. The doctor makes his calls by plane!

73 The Ashes, generally believed to be those of a stump or bail, contained in a trophy which is on permanent display at Lord's. England and Australia compete for the Ashes in the Test Match series, but the winner does not actually hold the trophy.

74 This phrase was made famous by the Australian poet, A. B. Paterson, and means carrying or humping your bag or pack (Matilda) which is jogging up and down to your steps (waltzing).

75 Canberra.

76 Snowy.

77 Walkabout.

78 Tasmania.

79 Sheep.

80 Marsupial.

81 Anzac (which stands for Australian and New Zealand Army Corps).

82 Bondi.

83 Swagman.

84 Morris dancing.

85 Flamenco. It was the dance of the gypsies who travelled from the East to Spain many years ago.

86 The hornpipe. It was originally accompanied by a wooden pipe with a horn at one end.

87 The hula hula. The women often wear garlands of flowers and raffia skirts.

88 The Charleston.

89 A short dress with stiffened frills.

90 The person who creates dances.

91 Dancing on the tips of one's toes. Special shoes must be worn for this and it can cause damage if attempted too early.

92 Nothing. Ballet shoes have no set right and left feet until the dancer decides which feels best.

93 They keep the muscles warm and help prevent them from becoming stiff.

94 *Swan Lake.*

95 *Coppelia.*

96 *The Nutcracker.*

97   *The Tales of Beatrix Potter*, which was choreographed by Sir Frederick Ashton who also played Mrs Tiggywinkle. A film was made of the ballet.

98   *Petrushka.*

99   Rudolf Nureyev when he was a guest on 'The Muppet Show'.

100   Wayne Sleep.

101   Dame Margot Fonteyn.

102   Gene Kelly.

103   Isadora Duncan.

104   (a) Square dance; (b) Tap dance; (c) Can Can; (d) Scottish reel; (e) Rock 'n' Roll.

105   Static electricity, a charge produced by rubbing two different materials against each other.

106   The horse. A unit of horsepower is equal to the raising of 33,000 lb one foot high in one minute. Watt adopted it after working with dray horses, and it is actually about 50 per cent more than an average horse can sustain for one day.

107   Benjamin Franklin. He conducted a dangerous experiment which involved flying a kite in a storm to establish this fact.

108   Brown.

109   Uranium, as it is capable of nuclear fission. 1 lb of uranium yields as much energy as 33 million lb of coal.

110   The energy of falling water is used to generate electricity. It is a cheap power source in mountainous areas with high rainfall.

111   A small steak. Energy value in food is measured in calories. An ounce of lettuce contains three calories whereas an ounce of rump steak contains sixty-two. So, even a small steak would contain more calories than twenty lettuces.

112   Help, I've got a spanner in the works.

113   On your palm. It stretches horizontally from beneath your little finger.

114   You wouldn't. Your Valentine is supposed to be kept guessing!

115   He or she would fall in love.

116 Georgie Porgie.

117 Oliver Cromwell. He also closed theatres and banned dancing.

118 Friday's child.

119 'Sealed With A Loving Kiss' and 'Hope Our Love Lasts And Never Dies'. Aaahh!

120 The 'marriage' finger is the third finger (the one next to the little finger) of the left hand.

121 Something borrowed and something blue.

122 Gretna Green. The elopers could marry without licence, banns or priest and only needed to declare their intentions before witnesses.

123 They paid a pig one shilling for the ring at the end of his nose.

124 The celebratory meal usually eaten after the wedding.

125 The Royal Wedding of Prince Charles and Lady Diana Spencer.

126 Twenty-five years.

127 Worzel Gummidge.

128 Rudolf Valentino.

129 Adam and Eve.

130 The Taj Mahal at Agra, built by Shah Jehan in memory of his wife.

131 Catherine Earnshaw and Heathcliff.

132 Robin Hood.

133 Superman.

134 Romeo and Juliet; Lancelot and Guinevere; Bonnie and Clyde; Anthony and Cleopatra; Napoleon and Josephine.

135 (a) mandible; (b) sternum; (c) clavicle; (d) vertebra; (e) humerus; (f) ribs; (g) pelvis; (h) patella.

136 False. They are caused by viruses.

137 True. The last barber–surgeon in London is said to have been Mr Middleditch who died in 1821. The red and white pole, symbolic of barbers' shops, represents their old practice of blood-letting.

138   True. Pupils are like the apertures in a camera. If it becomes darker, they become bigger to let in more light.

139   True. It is about 2–3 per cent of an adult's body weight.

140   False. A balanced diet consists of proteins, carbohydrates, fats, vitamins and minerals according to a person's needs.

141   False. Colours can be seen but certain colours may be confused, usually among the red-blue-green range. Plugs are now wired in green/yellow, brown and blue instead of green, red and black to prevent sufferers from making mistakes.

142   False. A stethoscope is used to listen to the heart or lungs.

143   True. In 1928 he found a mould killing harmful bacteria in one of his experiment dishes. He developed it into the first antibiotic and called it penicillin. During the Second World War it saved many lives.

144   True. The average quantity of iron it contains is about 4.5 grams.

145   True. In herbivores (creatures that don't eat meat, only plant matter) they are even longer!

146   False. It beats more quickly.

147   True.

148   Yes.

149   They're all the same size.

150   *The Diary of Anne Frank.*

151   *The Secret Diary of Adrian Mole, aged 13¾* by Sue Townsend.

152   The 'Hitler Diaries'.

153   *The Country Diary of an Edwardian Lady.*

154   The diaries of Samuel Pepys.

155   Carrier or homing pigeons were used as they could be trained to fly back home.

156   Rowland Hill, who introduced a penny prepaid-postage rate.

157   First and second class post, first being faster.

158   A.L.F. is the Automatic Letter Facer. It turns the letters the same way up, reads the stamps and piles the letters in stacks ready for sorting.

159 If you don't know yours you can find out from your local post office. The postcode helps to speed up the delivery of the mail.

160 He received the first transatlantic transmission – three dots, which is the letter S in Morse Code.

161 Telstar, launched in 1962. 'Active' indicates that the satellite amplifies the signals it receives before sending them back to Earth.

162 They are both British satellite tracking stations.

163 Telex. This system is often used by business organizations as it combines the speed of the telephone and a visual record of the message.

164 It could be 'Big Brain' or 'Quiz Whizz' in your case, as it is the name that you choose to be known by.

165 W. H. Smith started his bookselling activities on railway station platforms and eventually developed a multimillion-pound business.

166 They are found in newspapers. A scoop is a story exclusive to one newspaper; a by-line is a journalist's name printed with his story; a leader is an article which explicitly gives the editor's views.

167 They are all journalists. Clark Kent (alias Superman) works on the *Daily Planet*; Marge Proops, the 'agony aunt' works on the *Daily Mirror*; Max Hastings of the London *Standard* won acclaim for his coverage of the Falklands War.

168 They were the B.B.C. radio services which became Radios 1, 2, 3 and 4 in 1967.

169 Breakfast television began!

170 (a) Puffin Books; (b) The Woolmark, the certification trade-mark for pure new wool; (c) British Rail; (d) No smoking.

171 Cymru (pronounced 'cum-ree').

172 Coracle.

173 Cardiff.

174 Coal.

175 Caernarvon.

176 Cardiff Arms Park.

177 Celts.

178 Cambrian Mountains.

179 Caerphilly.

180 Cardigan.

181 A dragon.

182 Welsh rabbit (or rarebit)!

183 The daffodil.

184 *Ich dien*, meaning 'I serve', the motto of the Prince of Wales, is also on the two pence coin.

185 Snowdon, the highest mountain in England and Wales.

186 Anglesey.

187 Offa's Dyke, built by King Offa in the eighth century.

188 Dylan Thomas.

189 Lady Diana Spencer.

190 Richard Burton.

191 Cliff Morgan.

192 David Lloyd George.

193 Aneurin Bevan.

194 Harry Secombe.

195 (a) Minstrel; (b) Fathers; (c) Harlech.

196 The Emerald Isle.

197 The River Shannon which is 260 km long.

198 The Giant's Causeway. The steps were believed to have paved the way to Scotland.

199 It is usually served hot with Irish whiskey and cream.

200 The Blarney Stone which is kept in the wall of Blarney Castle.

201 Eammon Andrews is the man whose job it is to surprise unsuspecting people for this television show.

202 Peat and turf are cut into bricks and used for burning.

203 Cut glass and crystal.

204 Limerick. The verse form is thought to have been invented by Edward Lear.

205 George Bernard Shaw.

206 The Eurovision Song Contest. Dana won it in 1970 and Johnny Logan in 1980.

207 The shamrock.

208 A mountain range in County Kerry.

209 There are no snakes in Ireland. Legend has it that they were all driven out by St Patrick.

210 Hurley, a game very similar to hockey.

211 Fifteen.

212 The harp.

213 It is a gathering of people where singing and dancing take place.

214 It is a cudgel made from blackthorn or oak named after a town in Wicklow. It was originally used as a weapon.

215 (a) Tipperary; (b) Irish; (c) Galway.

216 Leprechaun.

217 Nine days.

218 At midnight.

219 The letter X.

220 300 centimetres.

221 22.00 hours.

222 Wednesday.

223 The last year of a century can only be a leap year if it is divisible by 400. Therefore 1800 and 1900 were not leap years but 2000 will be.

224 July.

225 Red and yellow.

226 Greenwich Mean Time.

227 Fifty-two.

228 333.

229 One hundred. (There are many types of centipede, some having far more and some having far fewer than a hundred legs.)

230 Eight.

231 Six.

232 10,000.

233 Value added tax.

234 The Duke of Wellington.

235 10,000.

236 Wait for no man.

237 Autumn.

238 A long-playing record.

239 Eighty days. Phileas Fogg is the hero of *Around the World in Eighty Days*, a book written by Jules Verne.

240 A cuckoo clock.

241 Switzerland.

242 (a) 2 o'clock; (b) 11 o'clock; (c) 3 o'clock.

243 Peter in *The Tale of Peter Rabbit* by Beatrix Potter.

244 Bugs Bunny.

245 Brer Rabbit in the story by Joel Chandler Harris.

246 The March Hare, in *Alice's Adventures in Wonderland* by Lewis Carroll.

247 The Easter Bunny.

248 Hazel in *Watership Down* by Richard Adams.

249 Humpty Dumpty.

250 Egghead.

251 Cuckoo's egg.

252 Golden egg.

253 Curate's egg.

254 Dodo's egg.

255 Pancakes. For many years eggs were forbidden during Lent, so they were used up in pancakes on Shrove Tuesday, the day before Lent began.

256 During the church service on Ash Wednesday people's heads were marked with ashes in the sign of the cross, in memory of Jesus. The ashes were from small palm crosses kept from the previous year's Palm Sunday and burned as a symbol of grief.

257 He spent them in the wilderness, fasting.

258 The money is specially struck in silver pennies, two, three and four pence pieces; each person receives as many pence as the sovereign is years of age.

259 It is because Friday was the day of the Crucifixion and thirteen was the number who were at the Last Supper. When the two are combined, it is thought to be particularly unlucky.

260 Hat, flower, teeth, pattern round waist, hair, ear.

	Father	Mother	Young
261	cob	pen	cygnet
262	gander	goose	gosling
263	buck	doe	faun
264	ram	ewe	lamb
265	stallion	mare	foal
266	drake	duck	duckling

267 (e), (c), (a), (b), (d).

268 (c) has three squares and one diamond.

269 Where angels fear to tread.

270 In 1912 a skull was discovered in Sussex which was claimed to be half a million years old. It was later discovered to be a fraud. The Piltdown man was really an orang-outang.

271 Yellow.

272 Follies are extravagant buildings that appear to have little practical use.

273 Nothing!

274 Every year. 1 January begins the year and Christmas Day comes near the end.

275 From the paper used as a cone to place on a dunce's head. It was called a fool's cap.

276 He would have had difficulty eating anything in 1597 as he had been dead for fifty years!

277 It is a fish called a bummalo which is dried and eaten with curries.

278 A fisherman. They are types of floats.

279 Squirrels do not lay eggs.

280 A fruit-picker. Tree-shakers are used to harvest fruits such as plums and cherries.

281 Marsh-mallow is a plant found in marshy areas. Its roots were once used to make marshmallow sweets, but now these are made synthetically.

282 Charles I.

283 It is a sunken wall surrounding a garden or park.

284 With great difficulty as they do not have any milk!

285 Elbow grease is a term used to describe hard physical work. It is not an actual substance.

286 (a) A man on stilts.
    (b) Two people in a wheelbarrow race.
    (c) Someone wearing flippers.
    (d) Two people competing in a three-legged race.

287 This was the nickname given to James I.

288 Bikini Atoll is in the Marshall Islands in the Pacific Ocean. It was the site of U.S. atomic tests from 1946 to 1958. Its name was used to describe the 'explosive' effect of the two-piece swimsuit when it first became fashionable.

289 Of course! A house can't jump.

290 In 1752. When the Gregorian calendar replaced the Julian calendar eleven days were dropped.

291 Clown (b) is the odd one out. The character is Pantaloon.

292 *Macbeth.*

293 *A Midsummer Night's Dream.*

294 *Romeo and Juliet.*

295 *Julius Caesar.*

296 *Hamlet, Prince of Denmark.*

297 (a) 'Beware the ides of March' (*Julius Caesar*).
    (b) 'Something is rotten in the state of Denmark' (*Hamlet*).
    (c) 'Double, double toil and trouble' (*Macbeth*).
    (d) 'O Romeo, Romeo! wherefore art thou Romeo?' (*Romeo and Juliet*).
    (e) 'I know a bank whereon the wild thyme blows' (*A Midsummer Night's Dream*).

298 Mime.

299 The circus.

300 Pantomime.

301 Punch and Judy.

302 A Passion play in which the life of Christ is told.

303 The Globe Theatre, built in 1598.

304 The Stratford Memorial Theatre.

305 The R.S.C. performs in the arts complex called the Barbican.

306 The National Theatre is made up of the Olivier, the Cottesloe and the Lyttelton theatres.

307 Regent's Park Open-Air Theatre.

308 The names hidden in the star are Burton (Richard), York (Susannah), de la Tour (Frances), Olivier (Sir Laurence) and Rigg (Diana). The mystery letter is R.

309 Newcastle.

310 Northampton.

311 Canterbury.

312 Liverpool.

313 (a) Hadrian lived 76–138.
    (b) Lady Godiva lived 1040–80.
    (c) Henry VIII married Jane Seymour in 1536.

(d) Sir Francis Drake helped to defeat the Spanish Armada in 1588.

(e) Gainsborough lived 1727–88.

(f) Florence Nightingale went to the Crimean war in 1854.

(g) Decimal Day was in February 1971.

(h) Virginia Wade won in Jubilee Year, 1977.

314 Robert Baden-Powell, founder of the Boy Scout Movement, became Chief Scout at the first International Boy Scout Jamboree.

315 Dame Barbara Hepworth.

316 Frances Hodgson Burnett (1849–1924).

317 Josiah Wedgwood, whose factory in Staffordshire opened in 1759.

318 William Wordsworth (1770–1850), the poet who settled at Grasmere in the Lake District and wrote many poems inspired by its scenery.

319 Jane Austen, a clergyman's daughter who wrote about English middle-class life with humour and feeling. Her best-known novel is *Pride and Prejudice*.

320 Bath.

321 The Norfolk Broads.

322 Coventry.

323 The Needles.

324 The Lake District.

325 Stonehenge.

326 Cheddar cheese, Lancashire hot-pot, Yorkshire pudding, Bath buns, Dover sole and Cornish pasties.

327 They are all French cheeses.

328 All are French haute couture (fashion) houses.

329 These are French Channel ports – to which you might sail!

330 All are French makes of car.

331 They are characters in French stories. Quasimodo is in *The Hunchback of Notre Dame* by Victor Hugo, Alexandre Dumas wrote about the Count and Astérix is a comic character invented by Goscinny and Uderzo.

332 They are wines produced in France.

333 They are all famous French artists.

334 All are types of bread eaten in France.

335 Perfume. Grasse is the city in Provence where most French perfume is made.

336 Cookery. *Cordon Bleu* means 'blue ribbon'. The knights of Saint Esprit, whose insignia was hung from a blue ribbon, became known as cordons bleus; they were famous for their excellent dinners and thus the title became associated with good cooks.

337 Mustard.

338 Motor racing. It is a town in north-west France and a 24-hour Grand Prix race is held there annually.

339 Mineral water and spas.

340 Porcelain made from local clay.

341 Versailles. It was the seat of government for more than a hundred years and the place where the French Revolution began.

342 The Eiffel Tower. It is 300 metres high. Besides being a tourist attraction it is also used for telecommunications.

343 The Arc de Triomphe. It was built to commemorate Napoleon's victories.

344 The Louvre. It was opened to the public in 1793.

345 The Moulin Rouge (red windmill), a nightclub in Montmartre. The dance was considered very daring in Victorian times!

346 The Sacré Coeur (Sacred Heart). Millions of French people contributed to the building fund.

347 The Beaubourg or Centre Georges-Pompidou, in the Les Halles area.

348 Notre Dame. It was built on the site of a Roman temple and is dedicated to the Virgin Mary.

349 Dew.

350 Willow.

351 Wasp.

352 Puffin.

353 Nettle.

354 Elm.

355 May.

356 Yew.

357 Woodpecker.

358 Robin.

359 Nightshade.

360 Ear.

361 Rowan.

362 Nuts.

363 Skylark.

364 Kestrel.

365 Ladybird.

366 Daisy.

367 Yellowhammer.

368 Reed.

369 Speedwell, buttercup, cowslip, dog-rose, foxglove, bluebell, honeysuckle and snowdrop.

370 **Mary Poppins** is wearing Henry's hat, Sherlock's clothes and Charlie's shoes.
Bonnie Prince Charlie is wearing Sally's hat, Mary's clothes and Cleopatra's shoes.
Henry VIII is wearing Mary's hat, Cleopatra's clothes and Sally's shoes.
Cleopatra is wearing Sherlock's hat, Charlie's clothes and Henry's shoes.
Sherlock Holmes is wearing Cleopatra's hat, Sally's clothes and Mary's shoes.
Aunt Sally is wearing Charlie's hat, Henry's clothes and Sherlock's shoes.

371 The Quangle Wangle in the poem by Edward Lear.

372 The Emperor in the story by Hans Andersen.

373 Cinderella.

374 Pads or frames which used to be worn behind and just below the waist under the skirt to puff it out.

375 Long fur or feather wraps worn round the neck.

376 Trousers which are flared from the knee downwards.

377 To make your crinolined skirt stick out.

378 To raise your feet out of the mud.

379 To protect your legs from spatters of mud.

380 In 1850 Amelia Bloomer designed some loose trousers to wear when bicycling – they were named after her.

381 In 1947 dresses became longer, very full-skirted and decorative.

382 In 1966. It was designed by Pierre Cardin.

383 On your head. It is a hat.

384 On your face, but only if you are a man. They are very thick side whiskers.

385 On your arm. It is a type of sleeve with a very large puff at the shoulder.

386 ... yellow polka dot bikini.

387 ... lose its flavour on the bedpost overnight?

388 ... and you pull the damper out.

389 ... and a hula hula skirt.

390 ... and little lambs eat ivy.

391 Greta Garbo in the film *Grand Hotel*.

392 Humphrey Bogart in the film *Casablanca*. It is often mis-quoted as 'Play it again, Sam'.

393 Mae West in *She Done Him Wrong*. It is often misquoted as 'Come up and see me some time.'

394 Billy Cotton.

395 Arthur Askey.

396 Ben.

397 Tonto.

398 Hardy.

399 Elsie.

400 Abbott.

401 Lana Turner.

402 Ann Sheridan.

403 Jackie Coogan.

404 Tommy Handley. The title comes from the radio show 'It's That Man Again'.

405 Bing Crosby.

406 They are all dances. Whether they got them right or not you are sure to get a good laugh from the demonstrations!

407 'Jailhouse Rock': Elvis Presley (1958); 'Who's Sorry Now': Connie Francis (1958); 'Living Doll': Cliff Richard (1959); 'Walkin' Back to Happiness': Helen Shapiro (1961); 'Anyone Who Had a Heart': Cilla Black (1964); 'Good Vibrations': The Beach Boys (1966).

408 Etna, Vesuvius and Krakatoa.

409 Heidi.

410 The Pied Piper of Hamelin in the poem by Robert Browning.

411 Sherpa Tensing (a sherpa is a native guide).

412 Hannibal. During the trek he lost many of his 40,000 men.

413 The edelweiss in the musical The Sound of Music.

414 Snowdon.

415 Vulcan.

416 An eyrie.

417 The Andes in South America.

418 Spain and France.

419 The level above which snow never completely disappears.

420 As you climb a mountain the air gets thinner so the rays of the sun are stronger.

421 They are all passes through the Alps.

422 Kilimanjaro.

423 29,028 feet or 8,848 metres. You may score a point if you are within 1,000 feet of the answer.

424 Incitatus. Caligula also gave him an ivory manger and wine from a golden pail.

425 Red Rum. He won the Grand National three times, in 1973, 1974 and 1977.

426 Pegasus, the winged horse. According to legend he was transformed into a constellation of stars.

427 The White Horse at Uffington. Tradition says it was cut in the chalk by King Alfred, but in fact it is far older and may date from the Iron Age.

428 Black Bess. She was Dick Turpin's horse in the book *Rookwood* by Harrison Ainsworth.

429 Black Beauty. He was described in the book of that name by Anna Sewell.

430 The authority in control of horse racing and breeding in Great Britain.

431 Racing over fences. The term originally described a horse-race over a natural course with church steeples used as landmarks to guide the contestants.

432 Polo, a game brought to England from India in 1869. Mallets are used to hit the ball and there are four players in each team.

433 A rodeo. Rodeos developed from the cowboys' work with cattle and horses.

434 Only three-year-old colts and fillies may enter.

435 Princess Anne was the fourth member.

436 Saddle soap; hoof pick; dandy brush; curry comb.

437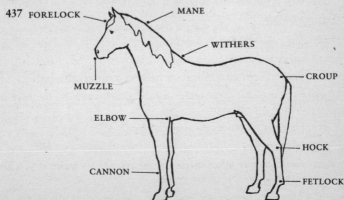

438 The Arab. This is the oldest breed of horse and is also said to run like the wind itself.

439 The Lippizaner. Foals are born black or brown and usually become greyish white as they grow older. They are known as the White Horses of Vienna.

440 The Shire. These were originally bred as war horses and had to carry men in heavy armour.

441 The Hackney. A horse with a distinctive high-stepping action.

442 The Palomino. This colouring may be found in several different breeds.

443 Pintos. There are two types: the Overo, whose coat is a solid colour with large white splashes, and the Tobiano whose coat is white with large coloured splashes.

444 Wally Kitson is riding Night Rider; Piggy Lister is riding Spotted Dick; Neville Starkers is riding Flash Harry; Mo Jersey is riding Grey Ghost.

445 Prince Philip, on 10 June 1921.

446 The Princess of Wales.

447 Prince Charles originally wrote *The Old Man of Lochnagar* to amuse the younger members of the family. It was published in 1980.

448 Prince William.

449 Prince Andrew. He was a helicopter pilot.

450 King John. His treasure sank in the Wash when a tide came up unexpectedly. The King John Cup, believed to be part of the treasure, can be seen at the Guildhall in King's Lynn.

451 Henry II. His words, 'Will no one revenge me of the injuries I have sustained from one turbulent priest?' had fatal consequences: four overzealous knights of Henry's court murdered Thomas à Becket in 1170.

452 Richard III. On Monday, 22 August 1485 at the village of Bosworth, Richard died while leading a cavalry charge. His crown reputedly fell into a gorse bush and when found was placed on the head of the first Tudor king, Henry VII.

453 Charles I was executed outside Whitehall Palace.

454 Edward VIII. He abdicated in 1936 and became Duke of Windsor. He was then able to marry Mrs Wallis Simpson.

455 Hampton Court was built by Cardinal Wolsey, whose father was a butcher. He later presented it to Henry VIII.

456 St James's Palace.

457 Osborne House in the Isle of Wight.

458 The Tower of London. Although it no longer houses these things it still contains the Crown Jewels.

459 Buckingham Palace. It was moved to its present position at Hyde Park in 1851.

460 St Edward's crown. The original was broken up in 1649 but the present crown does contain some of the original gems. The Queen leaves the Abbey wearing the Imperial State Crown.

461 His cloak.

462 A garter. The story is told that a lady dropped her garter and it was picked up by Edward III. Hearing somebody laugh he said, 'Honi soit qui mal y pense', which means 'Shame on him who thinks ill of it'. This has since become the motto of the Order of the Garter, an elite group of knights.

463 Queen Matilda. Her cousin Stephen laid siege to the castle and she escaped, camouflaged by the snow.

464 She usually wears hats off the face so that everyone can get a good view of her.

465 (a) Edward I was the Hammer of the Scots; (b) Richard I was the Lionheart; (c) Charles II was the Merry Monarch; (d) William I was the Conqueror.

466 Fourteen.

467 Sixteen.

468 Seventeen – but you must be accompanied by a qualified driver, have a provisional licence and display 'L' plates until you have passed your test.

469 Eighteen.

470 Twenty-one.

471 They protected the heads of the wearers, and also enabled them to gain a better view by standing on them.

472 German Shepherd or Alsatian dogs.

473 Identikit. Cards with drawings of individual features are put together to form a likeness of the suspect.

474 They are all types of fingerprint.

475 It is a lie detector, and might be used to test if suspects are telling the truth.

476 Dick Turpin, the notorious eighteenth-century robber.

477 Jack the Ripper, who committed some horrifying murders at this time.

478 Sweeney Todd, who used to kill his customers with a cut-throat razor.

479 Robin Hood of Sherwood Forest, who is credited with robbing the rich and helping the poor.

480 Fagin, in *Oliver Twist* by Charles Dickens.

481 Newgate. It was demolished in 1902.

482 Porridge – slang for a prison sentence.

483 Elizabeth Fry (1780–1845). She cared particularly for women prisoners and campaigned for better conditions.

484 Alcatraz, in San Francisco Bay. It was closed in 1962.

485 It is early release from prison.

486 (a) The pillory, an often fatal punishment as the hands were not free to protect the face from objects thrown by passers-by.
    (b) Burning at the stake, a punishment associated with witches.
    (c) The scold's bridle, a punishment for nagging wives. It was fastened round their heads to keep their tongues still.
    (d) The ducking stool, another punishment for nagging wives.
    (e) The stocks, a punishment for petty criminals where only the feet were trapped.
    (f) The cat-o'-nine-tails, a whip with nine knotted thongs. Its name was often shortened to 'cat' and the phrase 'not enough room to swing a cat' could have derived from its use in the Navy where conditions were often cramped.

487 The Pied Piper, in the poem by Robert Browning.

488 Alice in *Alice in Wonderland* by Lewis Carroll.

489 Charlotte the spider in *Charlotte's Web* by E. B. White.

490 The Greek forces led by Agamemnon entered Troy in this manner and destroyed it in a surprise attack.

491 Hercule Poirot in the detective story by Agatha Christie.

492 The *Mary Celeste*. The deserted ship showed signs of a hasty departure, but the court set up to investigate it could find no solution to the mystery.

493 El Dorado.

494 The Yeti or Abominable Snowman. The sherpas who live in Tibet and Nepal have long believed in these large hairy creatures and photographs have been produced of large footprints that are said to belong to them.

495 The Holy Grail. This was believed to be the cup used by Christ at the Last Supper.

496 Macavity, the mystery cat in the poem by T. S. Eliot.

497 The Wombles, who were created by Elizabeth Beresford.

498 Stig of the Dump in the book by Clive King.

499 The Rats of Nimh in the book by Robert C. O'Brien.

500 Professor Branestawm, hero of the books by Norman Hunter.

501 The Borrowers in the book by Mary Norton.

502 M.

503 Ra.

504 U.F.O.

505 Chan.

506 Brown.

507 Doctor.

508 Maigret.

509 Clouseau.
The mystery triangle is the 'Bermuda Triangle' (an area in the Atlantic Ocean in which a large number of boats have mysteriously disappeared).

510 Grand Canyon, Yellowstone Park, Disney World and Niagara Falls.

511 False. This event took place in 1773 when a group of men opposed to the import of cheap tea disguised themselves as Indians and threw a cargo of tea into Boston Harbor. This hostility was typical of the feelings that led to the American War of Independence (1775–83).

512 False. The financial situation which led to a collapse in share prices in 1929 ruined many people and became known as the Wall Street Crash.

513 True. The land was bought very cheaply and doubled the size of the U.S.A.

514 False. It was an imaginary line 'drawn' by two surveyors, Charles Mason and Jeremiah Dixon, which marked the boundary between the southern and northern states until the Civil War.

515 True. Calamity Jane's maiden name was Martha Jane Canary. This famous frontierswoman was a crack shot.

516 True. It was designed by a Frenchman, Bartholdi, and has been the U.S. national monument since 1924.

517 False. It is the name given to a group of prestigious universities which belong to an athletic league dating from the nineteenth century.

518 False. It is the name of a famous short speech given by Lincoln at the cemetery where the dead of the battle of Gettysburg are buried.

519 They were all Apache Indian chiefs.

520 Henry Deringer, Samuel Colt and Oliver Winchester were all fire-arm manufacturers who gave their names to guns.

521 One point for saying that they were all presidents, but an extra one for those who realized that their faces are all carved in the rock of Mount Rushmore.

522 They are all hamburger chains.

523 All these films were directed by Steven Spielberg.

524 They are all cartoon characters that appear in the *Peanuts* strip.

525 These are all rivers and states.

526 These gentlemen were all U.S. Army generals.

527 They were all American writers who have written children's classics: *Little Women, Little House on the Prairie* and *Uncle Tom's Cabin* respectively.

528 They are all film studios.

529 They are names given to students at different stages of their education.

530 These gun-slingin' gentlemen were all U.S. marshals.

531 A person who is friendly when everything is going well, but turns away when times are bad.

532 A promise to accept an invitation another time. It was once an American term for a baseball game ticket which allowed you to see another game if the original one was rained off.

533 Pisces, Cancer and Scorpio.

534 It is thought to indicate that bad weather is coming.
The rhyme says:

Red sky at night, shepherd's delight;
Red sky in the morning, shepherd's warning.

535 Run deep. It means that people who don't say very much might be thinking much more than you suppose.

536 An umbrella. Jonas Hanway (1712–86) was the first man to use one and was thought to be very eccentric for doing so.

537 It begins to rain.

538 It freezes.

539 The water evaporates and salt is left behind.

540 Hot breath on a cold surface causes a mist to form called condensation.

541 It stays the same.

542 It eventually evaporates and disappears.

543 In Gloucester, in a shower of rain.

544 On my head.

545 Mainly on the plain.

546 Down the water spout.

547 He went to bed.

548 A bath.

549 Mineral salts. They accumulate from the boiling of hard water.

550 Centrifugal force flings the water out through the holes of the drum as it spins.

551 Fluoride.

552 Approximately two thirds (65 per cent).

553 The colours of the rainbow are red, orange, yellow, green, blue, indigo and violet. The starred letters spell out the word 'gold' which is traditionally found at the end of the rainbow.

554 Chris Lloyd: tennis racket; Barry Sheene: crash helmet; Lucinda Green: saddle; Geoff Capes: shot for the shot putt; Jayne Torvill: ice-skating boot; Sebastian Coe: running shoes.

555 7.

556 90.

557 10.

558 15.

559 15.

560 0.

561 **Judo:** dan (degrees of attainment); hajime (the referee's instruction to begin a contest); shiai (a judo contest).
Fencing: lunge (a rapid extension of the sword arm to land a hit); parry (a fencer deflects an attacker's blade); riposte (a return thrust).
Cricket: bouncer (a short-pitched rising delivery); googly (an off-break bowl with a leg-break action); howzat! (a call to the umpire when the batsman is thought to be out).
Golf: eagle (two strokes under par for the hole); birdie (one stroke under par for the hole); fore! (a warning shout when the ball is struck).
Tennis: deuce (a score of forty all in a game); let (umpire's call when he says a point must be played again); tie-break (played in all but the final set when the score reaches 6–6).

562 Sue Barker.

563 Niki Lauda.

564 Ian Botham.

565 Kathy Cook.

566 John Curry.

567 June Croft.

568 Minnie the Minx, Beryl the Peril, Roger the Dodger and·
Dennis the Menace.

569 St Trinian's.

570 Billy Bunter, the hero of the books by Frank Richards.

571 Just William in the books by Richmal Crompton.

572 Grange Hill.

573 The Artful Dodger in *Oliver Twist* by Charles Dickens.

574 Jennings in the stories by Anthony Buckeridge.

575 The Elephant Child, created by Rudyard Kipling in the
Just So Stories.

576 *Pinnocchio* by Carlo Collodi.

577 Marmalade Atkins.

578 Squeak Piggy Squeak.

579 Hunt the Thimble.

580 Musical Chairs.

581 The Farmer's in his Den.

582 Kiss Chase.

583 Chinese Whispers.

584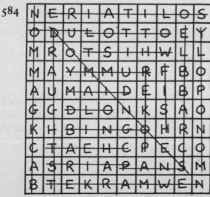

585 Cruft's. It was founded by Charles Cruft in 1891, but later taken over by the Kennel Club.

586 A small dog, bred for its looks and companionship. It does not 'work'. Many larger dogs have been bred down to toy size, such as the toy poodle and the King Charles spaniel.

587 It is the operation of cutting off some of a dog's tail. It is usually done when the puppy is a few days old for cosmetic purposes.

588 The governing body of dog breeders' associations in England, founded in 1873. Different countries have their own clubs and set their own standards of height, weight, colour, etc.

589 Mrs Barbara Woodhouse, a celebrated authority on the training of dogs.

590 A dog licence.

591 Nipper, who is pictured sitting by the horn of an old-fashioned gramophone on H.M.V. records.

592 Dog Toby, who had to bite or bark on cue in the Punch and Judy puppet show.

593 Nana, Mr and Mrs Darling's dog in J. M. Barrie's *Peter Pan*.

594 Greyfriars Bobby, a terrier who kept vigil in Greyfriars Kirkyard. His statue surmounts a drinking fountain nearby.

595 Luath the labrador in *The Incredible Journey* by Sheila Burnford.

576 Dougal, in the popular television show *The Magic Roundabout*.

597 Snoopy, one of the well-known *Peanuts* characters created by Schultz.

598 Toto, in *The Wizard of Oz* by Frank L. Baum.

599 Pongo, in *The Hundred and One Dalmatians* by Dodie Smith.

600 Tracking people. They have the keenest sense of smell of all dogs and can pick up a scent a week old.

601 To scent out game, track it and then stand absolutely still with muzzles, bodies and tails 'pointing' it out to the hunter.

602 They are different names for the same dog – a mongrel – bitzer this and bitzer that!

603 A blind person who 'sees' through his or her guide dog.

604 Either put it on his dog or wear it himself! It is the popular name for a clergyman's 'back-to-front' collar.

605 The Chihuahua, named after a Mexican state and city.

606 Sheepdog trials.

607 It does not bark.

608 The dingo. It is a menace to sheep farmers as it likes to raid their flocks for food.

609 (a) Spaniel, Spain: Barcelona Bounce.
    (b) Corgi, Wales: Cardiff Crunch.
    (c) Cairn Terrier, Scotland: Dundee Doggo.
    (d) Great Dane, Germany: Munich Munch.
    (e) Pekinese, China: Yangtze Yummies.

610 The Jumblies in the poem by Edward Lear.

611 Daisy in the song 'Daisy Bell' by Harry Dacre.

612 Tarzan.

613 Noah.

614 Doctor Who.

615 James Bond. It was designed for him in the film *Goldfinger*.

616 Mary Poppins.

617 The first all-steel, all-electric Pullman train in the world, the Southern Belle, was introduced by Southern Railways in 1933 and renamed the Brighton Belle in 1934.

618 A German high-speed diesel train.

619 A First World War biplane designed by Sir Thomas Sopwith.

620 A German airship.

621 The car that could fly and perform amazing feats. It was in the book of the same name by Ian Fleming.

622 The single-engine plane in which Lindbergh flew the Atlantic in 1927.

623   The penny-farthing was the nickname of a bicycle produced in 1872. The front wheel could be up to five feet in diameter and the back wheel as small as twelve inches.

624   Puffing Billy.

625   The Model T Ford, introduced in 1908.

626   The *Mary Rose*.

627   Concorde.

628   Sedan chairs were popular in the seventeenth and eighteenth centuries. Rickshaws were first made in Japan in about 1870.

629   Paddington Station opened in 1854, Liverpool Street in 1874.

630   The Royal Air Force was formed on 1 April 1918. The first jet-propelled aeroplane to fly was the Heinkel H E 178 in August 1939.

631   The *Q.E.2* was launched in 1967. The *Q.E.1* sank in 1972.

632   The vintage car goes to Beaulieu, H.M.S. *Victory* to Portsmouth, the Golden Arrow to Victoria, and Concorde to Heathrow.

633   Oliver Twist in the book by Charles Dickens.

634   The dormouse in *Alice in Wonderland* by Lewis Carroll.

635   The owl and the pussycat in the poem by Edward Lear.

636   Jeremy Fisher in the tale by Beatrix Potter.

637   Popeye.

638   Tigger in *The House at Pooh Corner* by A. A. Milne.

639   Henry King in the cautionary verse by Hilaire Belloc.

640   Charlie Bucket in *Charlie and the Chocolate Factory* by Roald Dahl.

641   The sandwich. The fourth Earl of Sandwich was a constant gambler. He ordered some beef between two slices of bread so that he would not have to leave the game to eat.

642   Frozen food. He first experimented with the process in the 1920s in the U.S.A.

643   H. J. Heinz. The first food he tried to sell was horseradish.

644   Barbecuing.

645 Tea. When it was first brought to England some people boiled it, threw away the water and ate the leaves!

646 Honey.

647 A kind of sausage made of blood and suet.

648 The soya bean. It contains a lot of protein and is a cheap substitute for meat.

649 They are all made into sauces.

650 They are all types of bread loaves.

651 Eggs are used in all these dishes: the yolk in mayonnaise, the white in meringues and the whole egg in omelettes.

652 They are all Greek foods.

653 These are all herbs.

654 These implements are used for draining and separating.

655 These are methods of cooking potatoes.

656 They are types of soup.

657 (a) hot dog; (b) fish fingers; (c) toad-in-the-hole; (d) fairy cake; (e) hot cross bun.

658 Blackpool.

659 Hastings.

660 Southend-on-Sea.

661 Dover.

662 Penzance.

663 Whitby.

664 (a) halibut; (b) mackerel; (c) haddock; (d) plaice; (e) skate; (f) salmon.

665 A starfish.

666 Ten.

667 As lobsters grow bigger they need a larger shell. Unlike skin, a lobster's shell does not grow with its body.

668 A pearl. Pearls are not proper stones, but are formed from the secretions produced round a foreign object, such as a grain of sand, as the oysters try to get rid of it.

669 Animals.

670 The Portuguese man-o'-war – jellyfish. It has a semi-transparent body that looks like jelly.

671 The Walrus in 'The Walrus and the Carpenter' by Lewis Carroll.

672 The albatross.

673 The Ancient Mariner in the poem by Samuel Taylor Coleridge.

674 The egg case of a skate, ray or shark.

675 Puff.

676 Punch, with his wife, Judy.

677 (a) limpet; (b) whelk; (c) mussel; (d) cowrie; (e) razor; (f) oyster; (g) periwinkle; (h) scallop. The family name is 'molluscs'.

678 Five.

679 1944.

680 Sixteen.

681 General Certificate of Education.

682 Yes – religious instruction and physical education.

683 He would learn how to make barrels and casks.

684 Sunday Schools.

685 Teachers would teach the most able or the older children. These children became monitors and then taught what they had learnt to the younger children. This system was a help in teaching large classes.

686 Eton College.

687 Rugby football. It was said to have originated at Rugby School in the 1820s.

688 The joint term for Oxford and Cambridge universities.

689 (a) a nanny; (b) an army officer; (c) a ballet dancer.

690 A sheet of paper containing information, such as the alphabet, was mounted on wood and protected by a transparent sheet of horn. These books were once used in infant schools.

691 Reading, 'riting and 'rithmetic!

692 The subjects and courses that you study at school.

693 Fifteen. It rose to sixteen in 1973.

694 Computers.

695 (a) first day of the month; (b) ... who's there?; (c) ... losers weepers.

696 'The happiest days of your life'. The code moves each letter forward to the next in the alphabet.

697 Yeast.

698 Wheat.

699 Breakfast. This comes from 'The King's Breakfast' by A. A. Milne.

700 Bread to which no raising agent has been added.

701 (a) Greece; (b) India; (c) Germany.

702 Salary. The ancient Romans gave an allowance of salt to the soldiers. Later, when money was given instead, the word 'salarium' was retained.

703 Water with a lot of salt in it. The sea is often called 'the briny'.

704 The Dead Sea in Israel.

705 Lot's wife.

706 An experienced sailor.

707 Caffeine.

708 Japan.

709 A Russian tea-urn.

710 The bud and two youngest leaves of a shoot.

711 The Mad Hatter and the March Hare in *Alice in Wonderland* by Lewis Carroll.

712 Paddy fields.

713 When you get married.

714 It is the staple food of a large part of the world's population.

715 Rice that is processed to remove only the husks.

716 (a) Spain; (b) Italy; (c) India.

717 Most sugar comes from sugar cane or sugar beet. In sugar cane it comes from the stem of the plant and in sugar beet it comes from the root.

718 Sugar and spice and all things nice!

719 It becomes a brown syrup called caramel.

720 The syrup remaining after sugar is crystallized out of cane or beet juice.

721 Icing sugar, then caster and then granulated.

722 Stilton.

723 Curds are the solids formed when milk is mixed with acid; whey is the liquid left at the end of this process.

724 It makes you look as if you are smiling!

725 (a) Switzerland; (b) Holland; (c) Greece.

726 Cottage cheese.

727 Brass, woodwind, strings and percussion.

728 Self-taught musicians 'play by ear'. They have no formal training and usually don't read music. A formally trained musician can normally play by ear as well.

729 A band in which the instruments have been made from oil-drums. The top of the drum is hammered into a pattern of different sized shapes, each of which makes a different sound when hit.

730 Music played by small groups of musicians, originally in salons or chambers. There are all sorts of combinations of instruments, but most classical chamber music was written for string quartets.

731 500,000 for a single and 100,000 for an L.P.

732 Compositions for three or more voices without musical accompaniment.

733 A set of five parallel lines on which music is usually written. It is also known as a stave.

734 A copy of a musical work which shows the parts for each instrument. A conductor uses a score.

735 The leader of the first violins.

736 Wolfgang Amadeus Mozart (1756–91).

737 Dame Vera Lynn, whose most famous song was 'We'll Meet Again'.

738 Ludwig van Beethoven (1770–1827).

739 Antonio Stradivari (1644–1737). A Stradivarius violin is worth a fortune.

740 Niccolò Paganini (1782–1840). Sometimes he deliberately broke a string on his violin to prove he could play just as brilliantly on three strings as four!

741 Elvis Presley.

742 Franz Joseph Haydn (1732–1809), who put a loud bang at the end of a slow movement in his 'Surprise' symphony (no. 94 in G major).

743 All are symphonies by Beethoven: the third, the sixth and the ninth respectively.

744 They are musical instruments.

745 These are all opera houses.

746 They are all conductors.

747 These songs were all written by John Lennon and Paul McCartney.

748 Each is the largest instrument in its section of the orchestra, strings, brass and woodwind respectively.

749 All are opera singers.

750 These musicals were all written by Tim Rice and Andrew Lloyd Webber.

751 Larry Adler: mouth organ; Louis Armstrong: trumpet; Jacqueline du Pré: 'cello; Andrés Segovia: guitar; James Galway: flute; Kyung Wha Chung: violin.

752 Hastings. It was won by the Normans under William, later known as the Conquerer.

753 Bosworth Field. Richard III was defeated by Henry Tudor (Henry VII).

754 Lepanto. The Turkish fleet under Ali Pasha was defeated by the Holy League fleet under Don John of Austria.

755 Trafalgar. At the beginning Nelson sent out his famous signal, 'England expects every man will do his duty'.

756 The Alamo. A Texan mission was the scene of the battle.

757 Gettysburg. This was one of the most important battles in the American Civil War.

758 The Somme. Many of the tanks were unreliable and broke down.

759 Samurai.

760 Crusaders.

761 Gurkhas.

762 Mongols.

763 Guerrillas.

764 Kamikaze pilots.

765 Nelson at the Battle of Copenhagen in 1801.

766 Queen Boadicea (or Boudicca). Her rebellion ended in defeat and she committed suicide in A.D. 62.

767 Tweedledum and Tweedledee in *Through the Looking-Glass* by Lewis Carroll.

768 Joan of Arc (1412–31). The judgment of the court which sentenced her to death was later reversed, and she was canonized in 1920.

769 Winston Churchill.

770 The Grave of the Unknown Warrior.

771 The Duke of Wellington.

772 Custer *v.* Sitting Bull; Napoleon *v.* Wellington; Cavaliers *v.* Roundheads; Wolfe *v.* Montcalm; Montgomery *v.* Rommel.

773 In A. A. Milne's story, Winnie-the-Pooh admits this to Owl as the reason for his confusion over long words.

774 Michael Bond's Paddington, the bear who took his name from the station on which he was found.

775 Baloo, in the *Jungle Book* by Rudyard Kipling.

776 Fozzie, Kermit's friend in Jim Henson's 'Muppet Show'.

777 Rupert Bear, originally created by Mary Tourtell, has appeared in a comic strip since 1920.

778 Sooty, the glove puppet created by Harry Corbett.

779 Yogi Bear.

780 Teddy Robinson in the books by Joan Robinson.

781 The polar bear. Seals are readily available in the Arctic regions he inhabits.

782 To help provide a grip on the slippery ice.

783 The Andean spectacled bear of South America.

784 The sun bear of South-East Asia. Its name derives from the yellow crescent on its chest said to represent the rising sun.

785 The grizzly bear.

786 In the adult bears' den between December and February.

787 The panda. It is thought by scientists either to be a member of the racoon family or a distant relative of the bear family.

788 The koala bear.

789 Ursa Major and Minor, two constellations in the northern hemisphere.

790 Davy Crockett.

791 Theodore Roosevelt. The teddy bear was named after him.

792 Their first names all mean bear!

793 Switzerland. The capital is Berne and has a brown bear on its coat-of-arms.

794 *The Winter's Tale*, Act III, scene iii.

795 Bear-baiting, a cruel sport in which a bear was chained to a stake and dogs let loose to attack it.

796 The Stock Exchange. The names apply to men who use different methods of making a profit.

797 Roo, Winnie-the-Pooh, Kanga, Eeyore, Piglet, Owl, Tigger, Christopher Robin. The message is 'Happy Birthday Pooh!'

798 Grace Darling.

799 Lawrence of Arabia.

800 Sir Francis Chichester.

801 Amy Johnson. She also flew to Tokyo in 1932, and to the Cape of Good Hope and back in 1936.

802 Robert Scott.

803 Marco Polo.

804 Dame Freya Stark. Her books include *The Southern Gates of Arabia* and *The Journey's Echo*.

805 Captain James Cook.

806 Robinson Crusoe, Sindbad, Biggles, Tarzan, Ulysses, Wonderwoman, Galahad, Superman.

807 Two.

808 Twice. The title of the film is *You Only Live Twice*.

809 Three.

810 Malta.

811 Belgium.

812 North America.

813 Australia.

814 New Zealand.

815 Russia.

816 Islam. Muslims make the journey to the birthplace of Muhammad.

817 Judaism. Boys, usually aged about thirteen, read aloud in the synagogue and are then regarded as members of the adult community.

818 Hinduism. Brahman is worshipped in hundreds of different forms, of which the three most important are Brahma, Shiva and Vishnu.

819 Christianity. Christening is the ceremony of naming by a priest with the blessing of the church and is usually accompanied by baptism with holy water.

820 Sikhism. Sikhs are given this name, which means 'lion'.

821 France.

822 Germany.

823 Britain.

824 U.S.A.

825 Italy.

826 Pesetas.

827 Drachmas.

828 Dollars.

829 Lira.

830 Rupees.

831 Dr Albert Schweitzer, who raised funds by organ recitals in Europe.

832 Anwar El Sadat and Menachem Begin.

833 Martin Luther King.

834 Mother Teresa.

835 (a) Egypt; (b) Spain; (c) Paris; (d) Rhine; (e) Nepal; (f) Tokyo; (g) Eiger; (h) Andes. The language is Esperanto.

836 The Grimm Brothers' witch in 'Hansel and Gretel'. She lured children into her cottage with the promise of sweet things in order to trap them.

837 Spike Milligan's Badjelly. Dulboot had ten eyes all around his head so that he could see behind him without turning round.

838 Meg, in the series of books by Helen Nicoll and Jan Pienkowski about a witch who is not very good at casting spells.

839 The White Witch in *The Lion, the Witch and the Wardrobe* by C. S. Lewis.

840 Miss Eglantine Price, a demure spinster and student of witch-craft whose double life is described in *Bedknob and Broomstick* by Mary Norton.

841 Ged, also known as Sparrowhawk, in *The Wizard of Earthsea* by Ursula Le Guin.

842 Gandalf, in *The Hobbit* by J. R. R. Tolkien, when he is chosen to be the fourteenth member of an expedition to regain the treasure stolen by Smaug.

843 The Wizard of Oz, in the story of that name by Frank L. Baum.

844 Catweazle, an eleventh-century magician who flies through time instead of space in the books by Richard Carpenter.

845 Merlin made it for Uther Pendragon who gave it to Guinevere's father. It came to King Arthur as a wedding present when he married Guinevere.

846 The Sugar Plum Fairy in the ballet by Tchaikovsky.

847 Titania (in *A Midsummer Night's Dream* by William Shakespeare) is bewitched by Oberon. When she wakes from a sleep she falls in love with the first thing that she sees – a workman called Bottom!

848 Crustacea in *The Ordinary Princess* by M. M. Kaye.

849 Tinkerbell. Peter saves her by asking children to clap if they believe in fairies.

850 Mrs Doasyouwouldbedoneby in *The Water Babies* by Charles Kingsley.

851 The ghost of Catherine Howard, the fifth wife of Henry VIII.

852 Banquo. The ghost is only visible to Macbeth, who was responsible for his murder.

853 The ghostly face of Marley in *A Christmas Carol* by Charles Dickens.

854 *The Flying Dutchman*, a phantom ship whose stubborn captain blasphemed as he attempted to sail around the Cape and was condemned to sail until Doomsday.

855 A ghost writer.

856 All Saints' Day.

857 Salem, Massachusetts, the scene of many witch hunts in the seventeenth century.

858 Trick or treat. Householders can opt to give the children a treat of fruit or sweets, or to have a trick played on them, such as putting soap on their windows.

859 Jack o' Lantern. This is a light made by highly inflammable marsh gas which led people to think they were safely near a town rather than dangerously near a bog.

860 Pumpkins, turnips or swedes which are hollowed out and have a lighted candle placed within.

861 Abracadabra, Open Sesame and Hocus Pocus.

862 Emperor Nero (A.D. 37–68).

863 San Francisco.

864 Pompeii.

865 Pudding Lane.

866 The R 101.

867 Sixteen.

868 Dynamite. He did discover others but this is the best known.

869 T.N.T.

870 Fireworks.

871 Saint Catherine.

872 The phoenix.

873 (a) blue; (b) yellow; (c) green.

874 Alphonse (Al) Capone.

875 Delilah, who cut off Samson's hair after he had confided that it was the secret of his strength.

876 Richard III. The princes were Edward V and his brother, the Duke of York. There is now some doubt as to whether the princes were killed by Richard.

877 Attila (c. 406–453). Only payment from the Pope prevented him from sacking Rome.

878 Jesse James.

879 Adolf Hitler.

880 Goldfinger, Bluto, Bluebeard, Captain Hook, Cruella de Vil, Darth Vader.

881 Cleopatra's Needle. It is one of a pair which were erected in Heliopolis in about 1500 B.C. Its 'partner' is in Central Park, New York.

882 The Monument. It commemorates the great fire of London of 1666 and its height is said to be equal to the distance from its base to the site of the shop in Pudding Lane where the fire started.

883 Trafalgar Square. Nelson's statue is about 5.3 metres high and commemorates his victory at Trafalgar.

884 Westminster Abbey. The Coronation Chair contains the Stone of Scone and every English monarch since Edward II (except Edward V and Edward VIII) has been crowned sitting on it.

885 Saint Paul's Cathedral. The architect was Sir Christopher Wren and the inscription, which is in Latin, says, *Si monumentum requiris, circumspice.*

886 Kensington Gardens. It is the site of the statue of Peter Pan, hero of the book by J. M. Barrie.

887 The Natural History Museum in Cromwell Road, s.w.7.

888 St Stephen's Tower. This is the clock tower of the Houses of Parliament. The bell is called Big Ben.

889 The Duke of Wellington. Apsley House is open to the public as the Wellington Museum.

890 Sherlock Holmes, the detective created by Sir Arthur Conan Doyle.

891 The Chancellor of the Exchequer, who produces the Budget and is responsible for the economy.

892 The Lord Mayor of London.

893 Charles Dickens, author of *Oliver Twist*, *Nicholas Nickleby*, *David Copperfield* and *The Old Curiosity Shop*.

894 Samuel Johnson, who said, 'When a man is tired of London, he is tired of life.'

895 Samuel Pepys.

856 Florence Nightingale.

897 Cockneys.

898 Turn again and become Lord Mayor.

899 The Ceremony of the Keys, when the Chief Warder and his escort lock the main gates and present the keys to the Resident Governor.

900 Fleet Street, where many newspapers are printed.

901 St Clement Danes.

902 The Bank of England.

903 The Notting Hill Carnival.

904 The City.

905 Starting at the Houses of Parliament the correct order is: West-minster, Waterloo, Blackfriars, Southwark, London, Tower.

906 (b) – the 'Gentleman Usher of the Black Rod' takes his name from the ebony stick that he carries. One of his duties is to summon the Commons to the Lords to hear the Queen's Speech. As a sign of respect for the independence of the Commons, he knocks three times on the door with the Black Rod before entering.

907 (a)

908 (c) – these meetings invariably take place in the central lobby.

909 (b) – Luke Hansard started to print these journals in 1774. His son later took over but in 1909 it became the responsibility of H.M.S.O.

910 (a) – Lady Astor became an M.P. in 1909 and remained in Parliament until 1945.

911 (b)

912 (a) – originally this office was formed to stop robberies in the Chiltern Hills. As it no longer exists and M.P.s are not allowed to resign from Parliament directly, this is a means of leaving.

913 (c)

914 (a) Winston Churchill, quote 2; (b) Benjamin Disraeli, quote 4; (c) Harold Macmillan, quote 1; (d) Neville Chamberlain, quote 5; (e) Margaret Thatcher, quote 3.

915 A thistle. The 'Most Ancient' Order of the Thistle was instituted by James VII of Scotland and II of England in 1687.

916 A spider. According to legend, Robert the Bruce watched a spider try and fail six times to fix its web. He apparently said, 'Now shall this spider teach me what I am to do for I also have failed six times!' On the seventh try the spider suc-ceeded and Robert the Bruce went on to defeat the English at Bannockburn.

917 Glamis Castle in Angus, the historic home of the Earls of Strathmore.

918 Harris tweed. Crofters shear the sheep, wash, dye, spin and weave the wool for the tweed in a secret way passed down through the generations.

919 A sporran, worn by men in kilts as they have no pockets.

920 Balmoral Castle, Aberdeenshire. Queen Victoria called it 'this dear Paradise'.

921 Burns' Night, celebrating the birth of Robert Burns. He wrote (amongst other things) 'Auld Lang Syne'.

922 Haggis. It is said to taste nicer than it sounds!

923 False. It is a train.

924 True.

925 False.

926 True.

927 True! Napier's Bones was a calculating machine invented by the mathematician Sir John Napier, who also invented logarithms.

928 True. Tam o' Shanter was the hero of Robert Burns's poem of the same name and the soft cloth hat is named after him.

929 False. They are smoked fish.

930 False. It is a dance.

931 Edinburgh, the capital city of Scotland.

932 Holyrood House. Holyrood means Holy Cross.

933 The Orkneys.

934 Loch Lomond.

935 Sir Walter Scott.

936 Ben Nevis, the highest mountain in the British Isles. *Ben* is the Gaelic word for mountain.

937 Caber.

938 Skye.
The monster's home is Loch Ness.

939 In the pantomime Buttons was traditionally Cinderella's only friend in her step-mother's house.

940 Nelson is said to have uttered the words 'Kiss Me, Hardy' before he died on board the *Victory*.

941 Chicken Licken, who met with other birds, such as Duck Luck and Hen Len before being eaten by Fox Lox and his family.

942 Robin.

943 Big Ears.

944 Artoo Detoo.

945 The Sundance Kid.

946 Boo Boo.

947 Gilbert and Sullivan wrote *The Mikado*. Gilbert wrote the words to Sullivan's music.

948 Rolls and Royce set up the manufacturing company famous for its engines.

949 Barnum and Bailey were fierce rivals until they decided to join their circuses together for 'The Greatest Show on Earth'.

950 Lennon and McCartney wrote the songs for the album *Sergeant Pepper*.

951 Tim Rice and Andrew Lloyd Webber wrote the musical *Evita*, based on the life of Eva Peron.

952 Flanagan and Allen were members of a variety act called the Crazy Gang. 'Underneath the Arches' was the famous song they sang together.

953 Woodward and Bernstein were the journalists whose investigations led to the uncovering of the Watergate scandal in Washington.

954 Alcock and Brown successfully flew the Atlantic in 1919. It took them 16 hours and 27 minutes.

955 Jayne Torvill and Christopher Dean won the World Ice-skating championships together in 1983.

956 Marks and Spencer started their famous chain of stores in 1887 with a penny bazaar. St Michael is the brand name of the goods sold there.

957 There are ten people hiding in the picture.

958 The Big Bang. The theory supposes that a single body, containing all the matter in the universe, exploded to form the galaxies, stars and planets.

959 A black hole. Scientists believe one is formed when a star collapses under the inward pull of its own gravity. This is called implosion.

960 A galaxy. It contains at least a thousand million stars of which our sun is one.

961 The whole of the sun's disc is covered by the moon, blotting out its light. Its corona (outer atmosphere) may be seen surrounding it.

962 The Apollo Programme. It succeeded in 1969 with Apollo 11.

963 The Space Shuttle.

964 The distance travelled by a beam of light in one year, at a speed of 300,000 km per second equal to 9.4605×10^{12} km.

965 It took place when the American Apollo and Soviet Soyuz spacecrafts docked together in space.

966 Planets orbit the sun and shine by reflecting its light. Stars are fixed and produce their own light.

967 Mercury.

968 Venus.

969 Earth.

970 Mars.

971 Jupiter.

972 Saturn.

973 Uranus.

974 Neptune.

975 Pluto.

976 Edwin Aldrin. Neil Armstrong was the first. The third man in the Apollo 11 mission was Michael Collins who remained in the command module.

977 Princess Leia Organa, as revealed in *The Return of the Jedi*.

978 Doctor Who.

979 H. G. Wells.

980 The cow in the nursery rhyme 'Hey diddle-diddle'.

981 Gustav Holst.

982 Yuri Gagarin.

983 Valentina Vladimirovna Tereshkova. She piloted spacecraft Vostok 6 from 16 to 19 March 1963, just 23 months after the first space flight by Gagarin.

984 Sir Isaac Newton – the man who watched the apple.

985 Edward Halley.

986 Brother.

987 Son.

988 Daughter.

989 They are brother and sister in the Topsy and Tim books by Jean and Gareth Adamson.

990 Cousin. They were both granddaughters of Henry VII.

991 Her son.

992 Nephew.

993 Step-sisters.

994 The March girls, the heroines of *Little Women* by Louisa M. Alcott.

995 The Marx Brothers.

996 The sons of Noah.

997 The Walker children from *Swallows and Amazons* by Arthur Ransome.

998 The Darling children who flew away with Peter Pan.

999 The Fonda family, famous American actors.

1000 The children of the Queen and Prince Philip.

1001 The Borrowers in the stories by Mary Norton.

1002 One End Street. These characters appear in several books by Eve Garnett.

1003 The little house on the prairie in the book of the same name by Laura Ingalls Wilder.

1004 Happy Families.

1005 Narnia, in *The Lion, the Witch and the Wardrobe* by C. S. Lewis.

1006 He was put in prison but later found to be innocent and freed.

1007 The English Civil War in the book by Captain Marrat.

1008 Rome.

1009 The Moomin family in the stories by Tove Jansson.

1010 (a) The Brontë sisters: Anne, Emily and Charlotte.
    (b) The Nolans: Bernadette, Maureen, Colleen, Linda and Anne.
    (c) Olivia de Havilland and Joan Fontaine.
    (d) Queen Elizabeth and Princess Margaret.
    (e) Joan and Jackie Collins.
    (f) Lulu (Marie Lawrie) and Edwina Lawrie.
    (g) The Mitfords: Nancy, Jessica, Diana, Unity and Deborah. (Nancy Mitford wrote *Love in a Cold Climate*.)

1011 George V broadcast his message to the nation on B.B.C. radio.

1012 A partridge in a pear tree.

1013 Three.

1014 It was the coronation stone from Scone, the place where the Scottish kings were crowned. It was taken to England in 1296 by Edward I. It was stolen from its place under the Coronation Chair in Westminster Abbey in 1950 and was eventually recovered in Arbroath.

1015 Tiny Tim in *A Christmas Carol* by Charles Dickens.

1016 Father Christmas – who was worn out by the trials and tribulations of his day.

1017 A plum.

1018 (a) hat; (b) angels; (c) pudding; (d) pear; (e) yuletide; (f) carols; (g) holly; (h) Rudolph; (i) inn; (j) star; (k) tree; (l) mistletoe; (m) advent; (n) stocking.
    The first letters of the answers spell HAPPY CHRISTMAS.

Heard about the Puffin Club?

... it's a way of finding out more about Puffin books and authors, of winning prizes (in competitions), sharing jokes, a secret code, and perhaps seeing your name in print! When you join you get a copy of our magazine, *Puffin Post*, sent to you four times a year, a badge and a membership book.

For details of subscription and an application form, send a stamped addressed envelope to:

The Puffin Club Dept A
Penguin Books Limited
Bath Road
Harmondsworth
Middlesex UB7 0DA

and if you live in Australia, please write to:

The Australian Puffin Club
Penguin Books Australia Limited
P.O. Box 257
Ringwood
Victoria 3134